sona BOOKS

© Danann Media Publishing Limited 2024

First published in the UK by Sona Books, an imprint of Danann Media Publishing Limited

WARNING: For private domestic use only, any unauthorised copying, hiring, lending or public performance of this book is illegal.

CAT NO: **SON0601**

Written by: **Adrian Besley**
Book design: **Darren Grice**
Editor: **Martin Corteel**
Proof reader: **Cameron Thurlow**

Cover images: **Getty Images**
Photographs: **All copyrights and trademarks are recognised and respected**

All rights reserved. No part of this title may be reproduced or transmitted in any material form (including photocopying or storing it in any medium by electronic means and whether or not transiently or incidentally to some other use of this publication) without the written permission of the copyright owner, except in accordance with the provisions of the Copyright, Designs and Patents Act 1988. Applications for the copyright owner's written permission should be addressed to the publisher.

The moral right of Adrian Besley to be identified as the author of this work has been asserted by him in accordance with the Copyright, Designs and Patents Act 1988.

Printed in EU

ISBN: **978-1-915343-60-4**

*FIFA Men's World Rankings in this book are accurate as of 15 February 2024

THE HISTORY OF THE
EUROPEAN CHAMPIONSHIP

Adrian Besley

sona
BOOKS

CONTENTS

INTRODUCTION 8

LEGENDS OF THE EUROPEAN CHAMPIONSHIP 10

Dragan Džajić/Günter Netzer **12**
Antonín Panenka/Wilfried van Moer **13**
Michel Platini/Marco van Basten **14**
Peter Schmeichel/Paolo Maldini **15**
Laurent Blanc/Iker Casillas **16**
Andrés Iniesta/Cristiano Ronaldo **17**

PREVIEW OF EURO 2024 18

Welcome to Germany – The Venues **20**
Euro 2024 Qualifiers **22**
Euro 2024 Play-offs **22**

MEET THE TEAMS 24

GROUP A 26
Germany **28** • Scotland **29** • Hungary **30** • Switzerland **31**

GROUP B 32
Spain **34** • Croatia **35** • Italy **36** • Albania **37**

GROUP C 38
Slovenia **40** • Denmark **41** • Serbia **42** • England **43**

GROUP D 44
Poland **46** • Netherlands **47** • Austria **48** • France **49**

GROUP E 50
Belgium **52** • Slovakia **53** • Romania **54** • Ukraine **55**

GROUP F 56
Turkey **58** • Georgia **59** • Portugal **60** • Czech Republic **61**

THE HISTORY OF THE EUROPEAN CHAMPIONSHIP 62

European Nations' Cup 1960 France **64**
European Nations' Cup 1964 Spain **68**
European Championship 1968 Italy **72**
European Championship 1972 Belgium **76**
European Championship 1976 Yugoslavia **80**
European Championship 1980 Italy **84**
European Championship 1984 France **88**
European Championship 1988 West Germany **92**
European Championship 1992 Sweden **96**
Euro 96 England **100**
Euro 2000 Belgium/Netherlands **106**
Euro 2004 Portugal **112**
Euro 2008 Austria/Switzerland **118**
Euro 2012 Poland/Ukraine **124**
Euro 2016 France **130**
Euro 2020 Pan-European **136**

THE HISTORY OF THE EUROPEAN CHAMPIONSHIP

INTRODUCTION

The 2024 European Championship is the 17th edition of the second most-watched football tournament in the world. It is a competition that has grown in popularity since the original competition in 1960 and now features 24 of the best teams on the continent. Over 2.5 million people have tickets to see the 51 matches in Germany, while around five billion are going to be watching live around the globe.

This book provides detailed previews of all the teams in Euro 2024, including profiles of the game's superstars and those who hope to shine in the tournament. It also tells the story of the European Championship itself, which was a long-held dream of Henri Delaunay, who, in 1954, became the first General Secretary of UEFA. It focuses on each tournament as it developed from a four-team 'European Nation's Cup' ignored by many of the continent's major countries to include eight teams in 1980. Then, from 1996, as 'the Euros' it became a tournament to rival the World Cup as the number of competing nations increased to 16 teams, before, from 2016, it reflected the popularity of the competition and welcomed 24-teams from across Europe.

The European Championship has always been an open and closely fought competition, where top teams have had to battle to progress. Only Spain have ever retained the trophy and even West Germany in their pomp didn't manage to win back-to-back championships, despite making three successive finals. Euro 2024 sees eight of the world's top ten nations compete to be champions. Stars of the game, including Cristiano Ronaldo, Kylian Mbappé, Rodri, Harry Kane and Jude Bellingham, will attempt to emulate legends such as Andrés Iniesta, Michel Platini, Paolo Maldini and Peter Schmeichel, who brought glory to their countries in previous tournaments.

The history of the European Championship is full of thrilling action, controversial incidents and incredible performances. It has heart-warming stories of underdogs rising to the occasion and heart-breaking tales of disappointment and defeat. It has heroes and villains, and has seen whole nations captivated, elated and dejected. There have been incredible goals, such as Marco van Basten's incredible far-post volley in a final for the Netherlands, Karel Poborský's exquisite chip for the Czech Republic against Portugal, and Ronnie Whelan's acrobatic effort for the Republic of Ireland against the Soviet Union.

In fact, the tournaments have produced many amazing moments. These include Dieter Müller scoring a hat-trick on his debut to cap West Germany's semi-final comeback in 1976; Paul Gascoigne's goal and celebration against Scotland in 1996; the Icelandic fans' deafening Viking Thunder Clap in 2016; the Netherlands' masterclass in 2000 as they destroyed Yugoslavia 6-1; and injured Ronaldo's tears as he watched Portugal's 2016 triumph from the sidelines.

Taking part in Euro 2024 are France, England, Belgium and a handful of other nations with real ambitions of lifting the cherished Henri Delaunay trophy. However, this is the tournament where anything can happen. After all, a team who had failed to qualify ended up winning the trophy; another team reached the final on a semi-final coin-toss; eventual winners have been in the position of losing the final with just seconds left to play; and 150-1 outsiders have surprised absolutely everyone by taking the crown. Bring on Euro 2024!

THE HISTORY OF THE EUROPEAN CHAMPIONSHIP

LEGENDS OF THE EUROPEAN CHAMPIONSHIP

Since 1960, the European Championship has showcased the genius of football's greatest players, introduced stars of the future and seen heroes step up from nowhere. This is a selection of them, but there are many more worthy of inclusion, including Zinedine Zidane, Franz Beckenbauer, Dino Zoff and other serial performers or characters such as Karel Poborský, Bernd Schuster or Paul Gascoigne, whose performances illuminated a single tournament. All have played their part in the tournament's fascinating history.

LEGENDS OF THE EUROPEAN CHAMPIONSHIP — 11 —

LEGENDS OF THE EUROPEAN CHAMPIONSHIP

 DRAGAN DŽAJIĆ

Born in what is now Serbia, Dragan Džajić is one of the best left-wingers the world has ever seen. His control and skill on the run was mesmerising and his left foot was a lethal weapon at dead ball situations. He was the star of the 1968 finals. The British press called him "the Magic Dragan" after his fabulous lob sunk world champions England in the semi-final. In the final, his goal and his trickery seemed enough to give Yugoslavia the edge, but Italy hung on. He was the tournament's top scorer and named the best player. In Euro 1976, he was still bamboozling defenders, scoring and running West Germany ragged in the semi-final that Yugoslavia somehow lost, and again made the team of the tournament.

 GÜNTER NETZER

The West German team that emerged as European Champions in 1972 was full of stars, including Franz Beckenbauer and Gerd Müller. It was, however, playmaker Günter Netzer who most epitomised their free-flowing, carefree style. Netzer made his international debut in 1965, but injury and inconsistency had limited his appearances. In 1972, his time finally arrived and his accurate long passing and creative bursts from deep were crucial in linking the team's play. He was the conductor and maestro of West Germany's seminal quarter-final defeat of England at Wembley, provided quality passes to set up both of Müller's goals in the semi-final and was integral in all three goals in the final. At the end of the tournament, no wonder the French sport newspaper *L'Équipe* was moved to call him the greatest player in the world.

ANTONÍN PANENKA

Antonín Panenka was no one-trick pony. The midfielder made over 50 appearances for his country and appeared in two European Championships, playing in every game as Czechoslovakia became Champions in 1976 (where he was named in the Team of the Tournament) and achieved a third-place position in 1980. However, it takes something special to have a particular skill named over you and Panenka managed it the most crucial moment of the final. In the penalty shoot-out, Panenka stepped up as the fifth Czech taker; if he scored, Czechoslovakia would win. He ran up at full speed and shaped to shoot to the right. As the keeper Sepp Maier dived, Panenka took a small step and chipped it gently down the middle and into the net. A move since copied a hundred times, but never as deliciously as the original.

WILFRIED VAN MOER

The diminutive box-to-box midfielder might not be as famous as other Euro legends, but his story speaks of the romance of the competition. Van Moer was a star of the Belgium side in the late 1960s and early 1970s. Then in the quarter-final of the 1972 European Championship as Belgium faced Italy, he fractured his leg in multiple places. Van Moer's career went into decline; by 1980 he was 34 and hadn't played for his country for over five years. Incredibly, with Belgium struggling to qualify for Euro 1980 he received a surprise call up. He not only drove them to qualify for the tournament but, in Italy, he was an inspiration, showing brilliance and leadership and helped them to reach the final against all the odds.

LEGENDS OF THE EUROPEAN CHAMPIONSHIP

🇫🇷 MICHEL PLATINI

In 1984, with France hosting the tournament, the stage was set for the brilliant 29-year-old attacking midfielder, who had won the Ballon d'Or and had been named the European Footballer of the Year for the third successive year. He did not disappoint. His exquisite passing and supreme finishing were on display from start to finish. Platini almost single-handedly drove France through the tournament. He scored in all five of France's matches – a record nine goals in total – as they became champions; including the winner in their opening match against Denmark and perfect – left foot, right foot, header – hat-tricks against Belgium and Yugoslavia. His coolly taken, last-minute strike from two metres out won the semi-final against Portugal and his free-kick broke the deadlock as France overcame Spain in the final.

🇳🇱 MARCO VAN BASTEN

The far-post volley from the tightest of angles that sealed Netherlands' 1988 European Championship victory was an audacious piece of skill that wrote Marco van Basten's name into footballing history. The prolific striker with a knack of scoring spectacular goals started the tournament on the bench, recovering from an ankle injury that had dogged his season, but finished as its stand-out player. Only one of Netherlands' goals in the tournament was not scored or assisted by him. He got a hat-trick in the crucial tie against England and in the semi-final, against West Germany, he earned the equalising penalty and hit the last-gasp winner with an exquisite hooked shot. In the final it was his header across goal that set up Ruud Gullit for their first goal, before he delivered that unforgettable final blow.

PETER SCHMEICHEL

When Peter Schmeichel kept goal for Denmark as they lost all three matches in Euro 1988, it seemed the nation's golden generation was over. Four years later he inspired their greatest ever success as his saves throughout the 1992 tournament helped Denmark to a historic victory. He performed heroics to shut England and France out to help them through the group stage and defied Eric Cantona and Jean-Pierre Papin to help overcome France in the quarter-finals. In the semi-final against Netherlands, Schmeichel's save from Van Basten's penalty won the shoot-out and in the final, his amazing backwards-falling tip-over of a header from Germany's Jürgen Klinsmann ensured a clean sheet and saw him named Player of the Tournament. He played in another four European Championships, but Denmark never repeated the miracle of 1992.

PAOLO MALDINI

Stylish and elegant, and a superb tackler with immaculate positional sense, Paolo Maldini is arguably the greatest full-back of all time. He played for Italy in three finals – 1988, 1996 and 2000 – and although he never won a champions medal, he featured in the team of the tournament in them all. He was 19 when he made his debut in a pre-tournament friendly and kept his place for the next 14 years, until he retired from international football in 2002. In 1996, Maldini captained a team squeezed out in the group stage by eventual finalists Czech Republic and Germany, while in 2000, *Il Capitano* was part of a defence that conceded just two goals en route to the final, only to lose to a 103rd minute golden goal.

LAURENT BLANC

Authoritative, intelligent and calm, the centre-back they called *Le Président* is partly remembered because he always planted a pre-match good luck kiss on goalkeeper Fabien Barthez's bald head. Laurent Blanc made 97 appearances for France and made the team of the tournament in all his European Championships. He played in the 1992 finals where, surprisingly, France went out in the group stage and, after retiring from international football for a short period, returned for their Euro 1996 campaign. In the quarter-finals, he struck the winner in the penalty shoot-out and scored in their unsuccessful semi-final shoot-out too. At the age of 34 he was part of France's victorious 2000 team. He scored their opening goal in the tournament and the team conceded just four goals in the five games he played.

IKER CASILLAS

Spain's greatest ever goalkeeper made the squad for five consecutive European Championships from 2000 to 2016. Casillas did not play in the first or last of those tournaments, but from 2004 to 2012 he certainly made his mark. At his peak, he was almost unbeatable. In 2008, he kept clean sheets in all the knock-out rounds and saved two penalties in Spain's semi-final shoot-out victory over Italy. He went on become the first goalkeeper-captain to lift the UEFA European Championship trophy as Spain defeated Germany in the final. In 2012, after Italy scored against Spain in the opening match, Casillas did not let in another goal in the tournament, setting a Championship record of 509 minutes without conceding as Spain successfully defended their title.

ANDRÉS INIESTA

The footwork, vision and balance that made the Barcelona star one of the world's greatest ever midfielders was on full display in three successive European Championships. Iniesta was instrumental in Spain winning two successive tournament titles and he earned a record number of man of the match awards (shared with Cristiano Ronaldo) in the competition. He played every game for Spain as they became Euro 2008 Champions, while at Euro 2012, when Spain retained their crown, he was named man of the match in three different games, including the final. Four years later he was given the award yet again in Spain's opening contest and he played in all four of their matches. He retired from international football in 2018 after 131 appearances for his country.

CRISTIANO RONALDO

Even though he is set to grace the field at yet another European Championship, CR7 is already the undisputed King of the Euros. He scored on his debut as a substitute and has gone on to net a record 14 Euro goals. These include headers, shots from the edge of the area, tap-ins (one after a mesmerising series of one-twos), an impudent backheel and two penalties, as well as the semi-final goal that helped send Portugal through to the 2016 final. He has played in the most tournaments (five – 2004, 2008, 2012, 2016 and 2020), is the only player to score in five Euros and has made an unequalled 25 Euro appearances. In Germany, he is likely to add to many of these records and become the oldest outfield player ever in a finals tournament.

PREVIEW OF EURO 2024

Germany welcomes 24 teams to the 17th edition of the European Championship. All eyes will be on Kylian Mbappé, Harry Kane and Cristiano Ronaldo and other top stars as well as newly arrived heroes, including Jude Bellingham and Jamal Musiala. Watch out too for possible stars of tomorrow such as Lamine Yamal of Spain, Warren Zaïre-Emery of France and others, who grab their chance to impress in what promises to be a thrilling festival of football.

PREVIEW OF EURO 2024 — 19

PREVIEW OF EURO 2024

THE VENUES

Germany is hosting the 2024 UEFA European Championship in 10 state-of-the-art arenas. It is a nation with a wealth of experience hosting football tournaments, including World Cups in 1974 and 2006 and the 1988 European Championships, and a reputation for generating fantastic match atmospheres.

The stadia are situated in Germany's major cities, from Hamburg in the north to Munich in the south, taking in the Rhine-Ruhr industrial centre, Leipzig in former East Germany and the capital, Berlin. Unlike many tournaments, groups will not be constrained to any one area or stadium, with each group's games spread across at least four different locations.

FIFA rules mean the stadiums must be temporarily stripped of their sometimes now familiar commercial and sponsored titles. Among the best known are the now-renowned Allianz Arena, which reverts to the Munich Arena, and Leipzig Stadium, which loses its Red Bull prefix.

Cologne

Capacity: 50,000

An old-fashioned rectangular stadium rather than a bowl, FC Cologne's ground will host five group games and a round-of-16 tie. The concrete and glass building is distinguished by the towers at the corners of the grandstands which light up in varying colours.

Frankfurt

Capacity: 51,500

Eintracht Frankfurt's stadium, a modern bowl with a retractable roof, was rebuilt in time for the 2006 World Cup finals. It was the venue for the 2011 Women's World Cup final and hosts four group matches, including one featuring Germany, and a round-of-16 tie.

Gelsenkirchen

Capacity: 62,271

As a tribute to the mining tradition of host cub Schalke, teams take to the pitch through an artificial coal tunnel. The site of Wayne Rooney's red card in the 2006 World Cup, it will stage Groups B, C and D games and a round-of-16 tie.

Dortmund

Capacity: 81,365

Famous for its "Yellow Wall", the largest standing grandstand in Europe, which holds 25,000 fans, Borussia Dortmund's stadium hosted games at the 1974 and 2000 World Cup finals. It will stage six matches in Euro 2024, including a semi-final.

Düsseldorf

Capacity: 54,600

Built in 2002, League 2 club Fortuna Düsseldorf's stadium missed out on hosting 2006 World Cup matches, but features five Euro 2020 games, including the last quarter-final match. From the outside the stadium looks rather like a box on stilts, but inside it resembles a modern bowl arena.

Berlin's Olympic Stadium (Olympiastadion) at twilight.

THE VENUES — 21

Hamburg

Capacity: 57,000

The home of HSV (currently in Germany's League 2) and used by Ukrainian club Shakhtar Donetsk in the Champions League, Hamburg's Volksparkstadion was renovated in 1998. It hosts matches in Groups B, D and F and a quarter-final.

Berlin

Capacity: 74,475

Hertha Berlin's Olympiastadion is the setting for the Euro 2024 final on Sunday 14 July. The iconic venue witnessed the 1936 Olympics, Italy's victory in the 2006 World Cup final and Barcelona's Champions League final victory over Juventus in 2015.

Leipzig

Capacity: 47,069

The smallest of the Euro 2024 venues, the home of RB Leipzig was once the biggest stadium in the former East Germany. It was rebuilt for the 2006 World Cup finals with the new stadium constructed inside the bowl of the old Zentralstadion.

Munich

Capacity: 75,000

Home to Bundesliga giants Bayern Munich, this stadium is hosting six matches, including the opening game and one of the semi-finals. It has a distinctive futuristic appearance and an outer skin of panels that can be programmed to light up in any colour.

Stuttgart

Capacity: 60,449

The home of VfB Stuttgart is still evolving and although the home fans' favourite Cannstatter Kurve and the swirling tent-like roof remain, it will have a new main stand in time for the Euros, where it hosts four group matches and the first of the quarter-finals.

EURO 2024 QUALIFIERS AND PLAY-OFFS

As hosts, Germany automatically qualified for the Euro 2024 finals, but the 23 remaining spots were fought for by 53 teams playing 236 matches over the qualifying tournament and play-offs, games that took place from March 2023 through until March 2024.

Portugal finished with the most impressive record. They won every single qualifying match, with a +34 goal difference and Cristiano Ronaldo extending his all-time qualifying record to 41 goals. **France** had a tougher group that included the Netherlands, Greece and the Republic of Ireland. Their only slip was a draw in Greece, but they did hammer Gibraltar 14-0!

The other unbeaten nations were **England**, who enjoyed home and away victories over Italy, and **Belgium**, who took advantage of an underachieving Sweden (as did Group F's second-placed **Austria**) and featured the qualifiers' top scorer, 14-goal Romelu Lukaku. **Romania** drew four, but won the important home tie with Switzerland, while **Hungary**'s double win over **Serbia** gave them the edge in Group G.

With Norway's challenge non-existent, **Spain** and **Scotland** qualified easily in Group A, while **Turkey** and **Croatia** found an inconsistent Wales no obstacle to filling the top spots in Group D. **Netherlands** shook off two defeats from the flying French to take a second spot and, similarly, **Slovakia**, who found **Portugal** too good, also managed to take the runners-up place.

Elsewhere, with no Euro place prizes on offer for those coming in third, many groups saw a desperate struggle for the first two spots in the group. In their final match, **Italy** only just mustered the necessary draw against Ukraine to finish second in Group C. Surprise package **Albania** finished ahead of the **Czech Republic** on their head-to-head record, with Poland squeezed out in Group E. Head-to-head results also separated Group winners **Denmark** and runners up **Slovenia** as Finland missed out.

Three play-off paths now decided the last three places available in Germany. Twelve teams were selected according to performance in the 2022-23 UEFA Nations League. The semi-finals in Path A saw two emphatic victories for home teams as Poland stormed to a 5-1 victory over Estonia and Wales shook off a disappointing qualification campaign with a thumping 4-1 win over Finland. The final in Cardiff saw Wales have the chances, but Poland stood firm. Even the penalty shoot-out was close with **Poland** winning on the last kick before sudden death.

Path B matched Israel, who had narrowly missed out on qualification, with Iceland, who only mustered 10 points in the qualifiers. However Iceland, with an Albert Guðmundsson hat-trick, produced a massive upset with a 4-1 victory in Budapest. Meanwhile, Ukraine scored twice in the last five minutes to defeat a shell-shocked Bosnia and Herzegovina. In the final out in Poland, **Ukraine** did it again. One down against Iceland, it took Mykhailo Mudryk's late winner to send them through.

The Path C semi-finals saw two teams who had struggled in the qualifiers benefit from home advantage. Georgia ran out 2-0 winners over Luxembourg, while Greece hit an unanswered five past Kazakhstan. An early red card for Georgia's keeper meant a cagey final, but **Georgia**, with home advantage, clinched the penalty shoot-out with Greece to reach their first-ever major tournament.

EURO 2024 QUALIFIERS AND PLAY-OFFS — 23

Romelu Lukaku of Belgium scores against Estonia during the UEFA EURO 2024 qualifier match between at King Baudouin Stadium on September 12, 2023 in Brussels, Belgium

MEET THE TEAMS

Twenty-four teams, featuring the continent's top players, emerging stars and promising youngsters, assemble in Germany for a Euro 2024 that is set to be closely fought from the outset. France and England begin as favourites, but as Greece proved in 2004, this tournament is as open as any and every one of these teams are there to compete.

MEET THE TEAMS — 25

GROUP A

Host nation Germany open the tournament in Munich. They are favourites to win their group, but if they want a place in the round of 16 they need to be focused from the off.

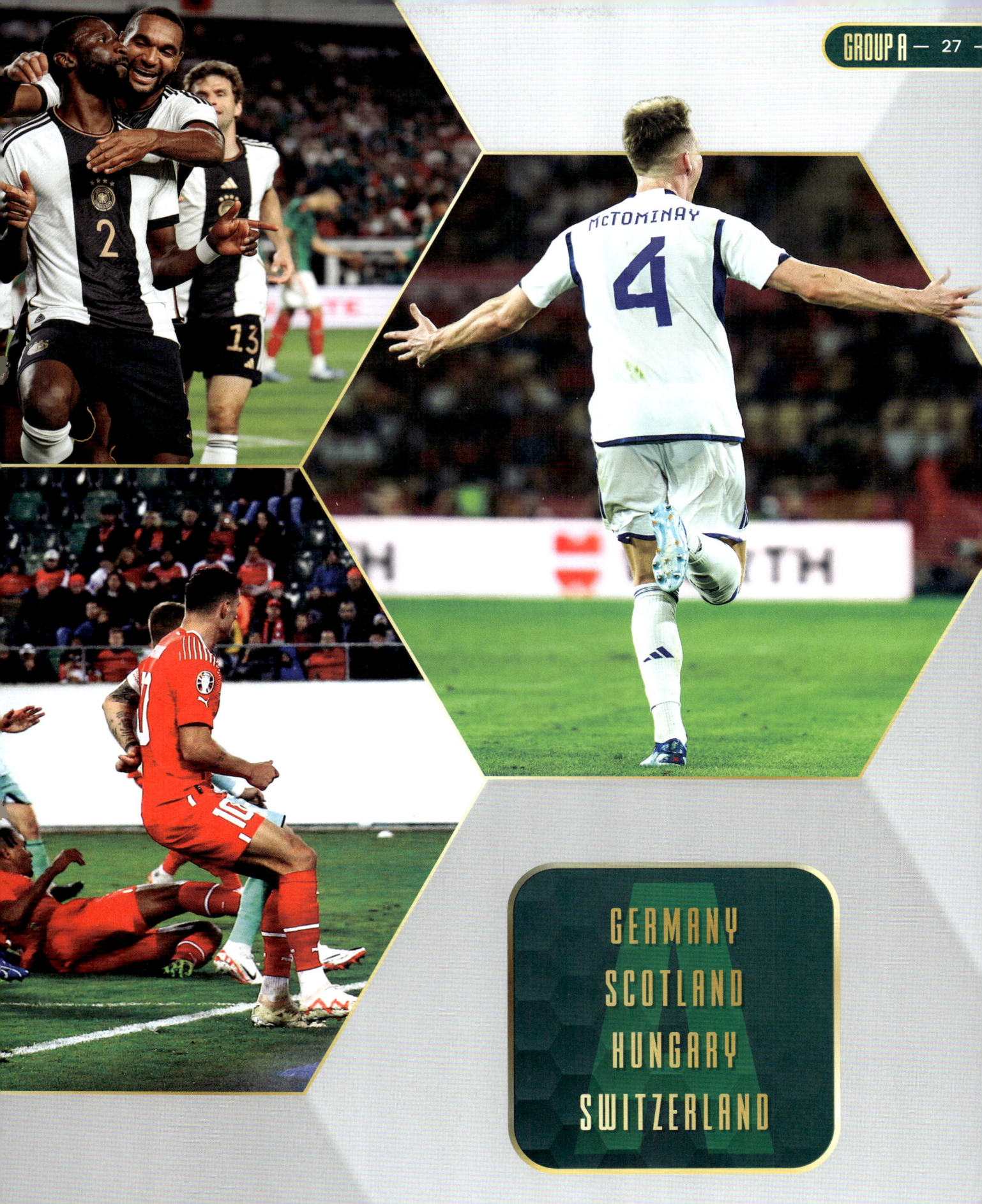

GROUP A — 27

A
GERMANY
SCOTLAND
HUNGARY
SWITZERLAND

GROUP A

GERMANY

FIFA WORLD RANKING 16
Colours: First:
White shirts, black shorts
Colours: Second:
All black, yellow trim
Coach:
Julian Nagelsmann
Captain:
Ilkay Gündoğan
Best European Championship:
Champions (1972, 1980, 1996)

Antonio Rüdiger (No.2) celebrates with teammates after scoring against Mexico in an international friendly

The host nation face their Euros with some trepidation. Not taking part in the qualifying competition means they have not played a competitive match since their disappointing exit in the group stage of the 2022 World Cup finals. Since then they have sacked coach Hansi Flick and appointed former Bayern Munich manager Julian Nagelsmann in September 2023. His task has been to find the balance, consistency, style and results that the team has been lacking.

In a run of friendlies, Nagelsmann has tried a range of different formations and line-ups. At the heart of the team he has so far kept faith with the team's senior players, including captain Ilkay Gündoğan, Joshua Kimmich and Leroy Sané in midfield, defenders Mats Hummels and Antonio Rüdiger, and forwards Timo Werner and Serge Gnabry. In addition, he has called on players from top clubs such as Jonathan Tah (Bayer Leverkusen), Benjamin Henrichs (RB Leipzig), Kai Havertz (Arsenal) and Niclas Füllkrug (Borussia Dortmund).

Nagelsmann has the personnel, but little time to find a team and a style that clicks. Will he be tempted to rely on veterans like Manuel Neuer and Thomas Müller? Or will we see him turn to some of the impressive young players he has available in Union Berlin defender Robin Gosens, Leverkusen's Florian Wirtz or Bayern Munich's Jamal Musiala? The German public were relieved to see the team drawn in a group from which they should qualify. Once through, in front of a home crowd, they have a chance of finding their feet and going a long way in the competition.

ONE TO WATCH

JAMAL MUSIALA

One of the world's most exciting young players, the 21-year-old midfielder's dribbles, assists and goals have thrilled at Bayern Munich and his magic is capable of igniting Germany's tournament.

SCOTLAND 🏴󠁧󠁢󠁳󠁣󠁴󠁿

Scott McTominay in action against Spain in a European Championship qualifier In October 2023.

FIFA WORLD RANKING 34
Colours: First: Blue shirts, white shorts
Colours: Second: White shirts, blue shorts
Coach: Steve Clarke
Captain: Andrew Robertson
Best European Championship: Group stage (1992, 96, 2020, 24)

The resurgence of Scotland as an international team began with the appointment of Steve Clarke as coach in May 2019. By way of the play-offs, he led Scotland to EURO 2020, their first major tournament since 1998. After coming bottom of their group, he then set about rebuilding his squad with young players. That cohort has now come of age. Just missing out on the 2022 World Cup and winning promotion to Group A in the Nations League, they qualified for EURO 2024 with two matches to spare and a single defeat in Spain.

Clarke has developed a tight-knit squad of young talent, guided by senior players, such as Kieran Tierney and Andy Robertson, and mostly playing in Europe's top leagues. They have a club mentality and with no out-and-out star players, they are very much a team. The highlight of their qualification campaign came with a 2-0 win over Spain in Glasgow where, courtesy of two Scott McTominay goals, they announced their arrival as an emerging side.

When Norwich City goalkeeper Angus Gunn declared for Scotland in March 2023, Clarke added a vital piece to the jigsaw and Gunn took his place behind a back line that includes Nottingham Forest's Scott McKenna and Jack Hendry of Saudi club Al-Ettifaq. The team's strength is in a midfield anchored by Brighton & Hove Albion's Billy Gilmour and Celtic's Callum McGregor. Aston Villa's John McGinn and Manchester United's McTominay (in a more attacking role for his country than club), often support a lone striker in Southampton's Ché Adams. A still improving team, no one will be taking Scotland lightly in Germany.

ONE TO WATCH

LEWIS FERGUSON

After a move to Bologna from Aberdeen in 2022, the 24-year old midfielder's consistent performances and regular goals have impressed in Serie A.

GROUP A

HUNGARY

FIFA WORLD RANKING 27
Colours: First:
Red shirts, white shorts
Colours: Second:
All white, red trim
Coach:
Marco Rossi
Captain:
Dominik Szoboszlai
Best European Championship:
Semi-Final (1964)

Dominik Szoboszlai (l) and Filip Krastev (r) battle during Group G qualifier between Bulgaria and Hungary in November 2023

Having made it to their third consecutive European Championship finals with a game to spare, Marco Rossi's well-organised side have belief and are confident they can top group A. The country whose Magnificent Magyars delighted the world with their brilliant football in the 1950s are due some success. They went 44 years, from 1972, without qualifying for a Euros finals and despite making the two most recent tournaments have failed to escape the group stage in both. Could this be a case of third time lucky?

They certainly have some momentum. Despite draws with France and Germany they had an unlucky exit from a tough group in the 2020 Euros, but a 2022 Nations League campaign saw them win in Germany and record a famous 4-0 thrashing of England at Molineux. Only defeat to Italy prevented them reaching the UEFA Nations League finals. Undaunted, they then went undefeated throughout 2023, including victories over Serbia, Bulgaria and Lithuania.

Rossi has a settled squad and has established them as a resilient outfit. RB Leipzig keeper Péter Gulácsi is protected by a strong defence, which features his teammate Willi Orbán, Parma's young defender Botond Balogh and Hoffenheim's Attila Szalai, and is patrolled by the team's most-capped player, Ádám Nagy of Pisa. They break quickly and in numbers thanks to Union Berlin's Andras Schafer and Barnsley's young attacking midfielder Callum Styles, while their two most gifted players are strikers Rolland Sallai (SC Freiburg) and Dominik Szoboszlai (Liverpool). This is a dangerous team who know how to get results and their Group A opponents will underestimate Hungary at their peril.

STAR PLAYER

DOMINIK SZOBOSZLAI

Since joining from RB Leipzig in 2023, Szoboszlai has quickly become a favourite at Anfield. He takes a number 10 role for his country and the gifted 23-year-old is highly likely to shine in Germany.

HUNGARY – SWITZERLAND

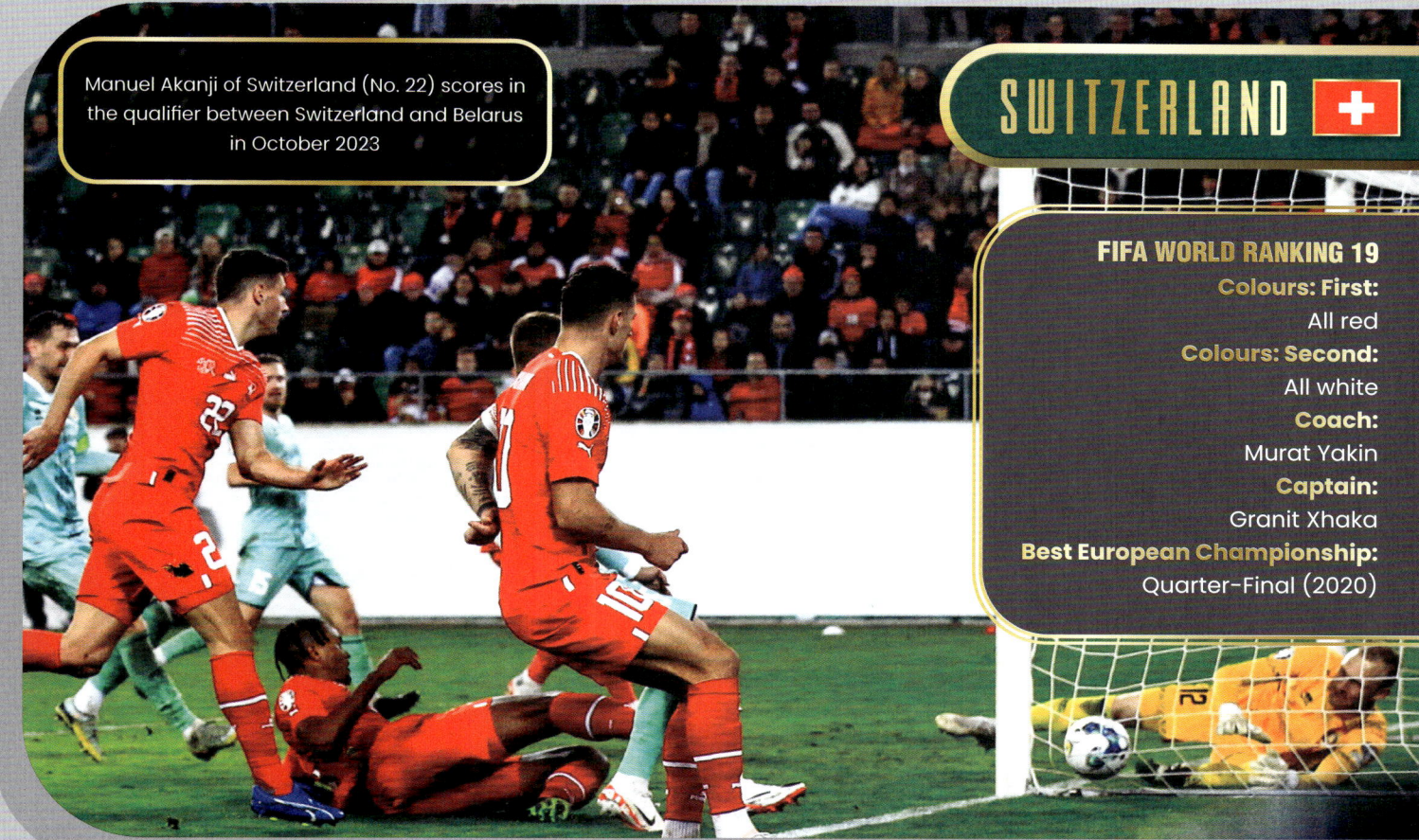

Manuel Akanji of Switzerland (No. 22) scores in the qualifier between Switzerland and Belarus in October 2023

SWITZERLAND

FIFA WORLD RANKING 19
Colours: First: All red
Colours: Second: All white
Coach: Murat Yakin
Captain: Granit Xhaka
Best European Championship: Quarter-Final (2020)

Since 2004 Switzerland have reached all but one of the major finals and have established themselves as a danger to top-ranking nations. In the last Euros, they reached the quarter-finals, knocking out France en route and taking Spain to penalties. Current coach Murat Yakin then led them to the 2022 World Cup, where they beat Serbia and Cameroon before crashing out in a 6-1 defeat to Portugal.

Qualification for the 2024 European Championships seemed to be a formality as the Nati, as they are known, went unbeaten in their first five matches. Then the wheels came off. They needed two very late goals to salvage a 3-3 draw at home to Belarus, could only draw with Israel and Kosovo, and just scraped second place to qualify.

Key to Yakin's team are former Arsenal midfielder Granit Xhaka and ex-Liverpool forward Xherdan Shaqiri, who each have over 100 caps, and Manchester City centre-back Manuel Akanji, who has made over 50 appearances for his country. The squad is not short of exciting players either, in the Bologna pairing of winger Dan Ndoye and midfielder Michel Aebischer, AC Milan forward Noah Okafor and Monaco's striking powerhouse Breel Embolo.

With a run of poor results and rumours of unrest among the senior players, Yakin needs to put in some hard graft before July. However, he has plenty of strong material to work with and his team could still progress to the knock-out stage.

STAR PLAYER

MANUEL AKANJI

The calm defender's reliable consistency as well as his pace, tackling and confidence on the ball have seen him develop into one of the world's best centre-backs.

GROUP B

With three teams ranked in FIFA's top ten, this is undoubtedly the tournament's 'group of death', but it could be in-form underdogs Albania's results that are ultimately decisive.

GROUP B — 33

B
SPAIN
CROATIA
ITALY
ALBANIA

GROUP B

SPAIN

FIFA WORLD RANKING 8
Colours: First:
Red shirts, black shorts
Colours: Second:
Light blue shirts, royal blue shorts
Coach:
Luis De La Fuente
Captain:
Álvaro Morata
Best European Championship:
Champions (1964, 2008, 2012)

Spain's Rodri battles with John McGinn of Scotland during the qualifying round match at Hampden Park in March 2023

After Spain exited the 2022 World Cup finals after a penalty shoot-out against Morocco in the round of 16, Luis de la Fuente, the under-21's coach, replaced Luis Enrique. He was a surprise choice and after a Euros qualifier 2-0 defeat to Scotland many Spaniards voiced their concerns. However, the veteran coach has slowly put his own stamp on the job, creating a more flexible approach such as using a conventional centre-forward. Quietly, he got results, winning every other qualifier, with the team scoring 25 goals in eight games and conceding just five goals, as well as triumphing in the Nations League final after victories over Italy and Croatia.

It might not be a classically stylish or tactically disciplined Spanish team, but de la Fuente has built a very effective unit. He has changed the spine of the team to lean on Athletic Bilbao's Unai Simon in goal, Real Sociedad's Robin Le Normand as principal centre-back, Manchester City's Rodri holding in midfield and Atletico Madrid striker Álvaro Morata as centre-forward and skipper. This has given him the freedom to field expressive footballers such as PSG playmaker Fabián, Athletic Bilbao winger Nico Williams and Barcelona's exceptionally talented Pedri.

Much of the pre-tournament talk has centred around two wonderkids, but they will miss the brilliant Gavi, Barcelona's 20-year-old star who unfortunately suffered a knee injury in November and is unlikely to be fit for the Euros. However, his teammate, winger Lamine Yamal, Spain's youngest international and youngest goalscorer, should make the squad. He is still only 16 years old and could be a big story in Germany. The coach is typically playing down Spain's chances, but don't be taken in – they are in it to win it.

STAR PLAYER

RODRI

The positional sense, tackling and passing ability of Manchester City's metronome are second to none and it is no wonder that he has become an indispensable holding midfielder for his country as well.

CROATIA

Croatia's Luka Modric vies with Wales' defender Neco Williams in their qualification match at Cardiff City Stadium

FIFA WORLD RANKING 10
Colours: First:
Red and white check shirts, white shorts
Colours: Second
All black with blue and black check shoulder
Coach:
Zlatko Dalić
Captain:
Luka Modrić
Best European Championship:
Quarter-Finals (1996, 2008)

Croatia booked a sixth successive Euro appearance with a 1-0 victory over Armenia on the final round of qualifying matches. As well as reaching the Nations League final (where they lost on penalties to Spain), they had a comfortable qualification journey until consecutive defeats to Wales and Turkey in October left them sweating. Coach Zlatko Dalić has been in charge since 2017 and has led his team to four consecutive major tournaments. They were finalists and semi-finalists in his two World Cup finals, but failed to progress beyond the round of 16 in two attempts at the European Championships.

Dalić's side will have a familiar look in Germany. Not only will talisman Luka Modrić – possibly – make his international swan song, but he is joined by experienced midfielders in Manchester City's Mateo Kovacic, Marcelo Brozović, the former Inter Milan hero now playing in Saudi Arabia, Ivan Perisic (if recovered from serious injury) and Hoffenheim forward Andrej Kramarić. With such a talented midfield at his disposal, Dalić won't change the team's playing style either; he is happy to play from the back with a 4-3-3 formation, creating chances through quick passes.

However, recognising he has an ageing team and in response to injuries, the coach has brought in some new faces and how they integrate will be key to Croatia's success. Defenders such as Manchester City's Joško Gvardiol, Union Berlin's Josip Juranović, and Ajax's Josip Šutalo and Borna Sosa are already settled, as is Atalanta midfielder Mario Pašalić, while many are eager to see Augsburg's young forward Dion Drena Beljo and midfielder Martin Baturina of Dinamo Zagreb, who has inevitably been dubbed 'the new Modrić'.

STAR PLAYER

LUKA MODRIĆ

He has over 170 caps, five Champions League winner's medals and was awarded the Ballon d'Or in 2018. Even at an extraordinary 39 years old, 'the magician' is still mesmerising to watch and is the key to Croatia's success.

GROUP B

ITALY

FIFA WORLD RANKING 9
Colours: First:
All blue
Colours: Second:
White shirts, black shorts
Coach:
Luciano Spalletti
Captain:
Ciro Immobile
Best European Championship:
Champions (1968, 2020)

Gianluca Scamacca celebrates with team-mates Stephan El Shaarawy and Destiny Udogie after he scores a goal to make it 1-0 during the UEFA EURO 2024 European qualifier match between England and Italy at Wembley Stadium on October 17, 2023

Defeat by Spain in the Nations League semi-final in October 2021 ended Italy's record run of 37 unbeaten games. What followed was a slump which saw the 2020 European Champions fail to qualify for the 2022 World Cup finals and they ended up in the lowest pot in the draw for the Euro 2024 finals, guaranteeing them a tough group. Halfway through the qualifiers coach Roberto Mancini bailed out and it was left to Luciano Spalletti, who had just led Napoli to a Serie A title, to rebuild a broken team.

ONE TO WATCH
DESTINY UDOGIE

The left-back's first season with Tottenham has been a revelation, and he has impressed in both defensive and attacking duties. Spalletti has already described him as a player who can 'make a difference.'

Spalletti has guided them through, but that is all. The team has displayed indifferent form and expectations remain low. He has attempted to introduce a more attacking 4-3-3 formation, but, like Mancini, is still searching for players who excel at international level. Beyond goalkeeper Gianluigi Donnarumma, Inter Milan midfielder Nicolò Barella and Juventus forward Federico Chiesa, there are few are team-sheet definites.

Spalletti finds himself looking to the old guard – players like Napoli defender Giovanni Di Lorenzo; midfielders in Fiorentina's Giacomo Bonaventura, Sassuolo's Domenico Berardi, Jorghino of Arsenal and Lazio striker Ciro Immobile – to help see them th rough as new stars emerge. There are plenty of possibilities, from Torino's Alessandro Buongiorno, Atalanta's Giorgio Scalvini and Tottenham Hotspur's Destiny Udogie in defence to attacking potential in Napoli's Giacomo Raspadori, Moise Kean at Juventus and Atalanta's tall centre forward Gianluca Scamacca.

The coach has created a good spirit inside the dressing room and now looks to build a winning team in the short time available. In such a difficult group he knows it is a tough challenge, but as he said after the draw for the finals, 'Never forget, we are Italy.'

ALBANIA

Albania's forward Sokol Cikalleshi (centre - partially hidden) celebrates after scoring the first goal in a 1-1 draw with Moldova in qualifying

FIFA WORLD RANKING 64
Colours: First: Red shirts, black shorts
Colours: Second: All white
Coach: Sylvinho
Captain: Berat Djimsiti
Best European Championship: Group Stage (2019)

Having made their first-ever tournament appearance at Euro 2016, Albania's progress stuttered until the appointment of former Arsenal, Barcelona and Brazil defender Sylvinho as coach in time for the Euro 2024 qualifiers. Sylvinho's first game saw a defeat by Poland in Warsaw, but his team gathered momentum and celebrated victories in the return against Poland and over the Czech Republic. They remained unbeaten for the rest of the qualifying matches, winning four and drawing three to finish top of their group and book their spot in Germany with a game to spare.

The new coach has brought in a 4-2-3-1 formation, which has strengthened the defence, and introduced inverted wingers, bringing right-winger Jasir Asani from Gwangju and promising young left-back Mario Mitaj of Lokomotiv Moscow into the squad. A strong settled team is built around Italian league players: in central defence Atalanta's Berat Djimsiti and Ardian Ismajli of Empoli have established a great partnership; in front of them Lecce's Ylber Ramadani is the holding player and Inter's Kristjan Asllani looks to bring the ball forward; while up front, Sassuolo's exciting Nedim Bajrami will worry many defences. They even have two of their best young players in Chelsea striker Armando Broja and Roma defender Marash Kumballa ready to return after suffering major injuries.

The Albanian diaspora is paying dividends for the national team as many born or playing elsewhere in Europe opt to play for their family's home nation. Albania might struggle to escape a difficult group, but their results could well determine just who else does.

ONE TO WATCH

ARMANDO BROJA

Still only 22 years old and brimming with talent, the English-born striker can hopefully recapture the scintillating form he showed before sitting out nearly a whole year with a knee injury.

GROUP C

If England play like possible champions from the off, the group could be a fascinating scramble for second place with Denmark most likely, but not guaranteed, to progress.

GROUP C — 39

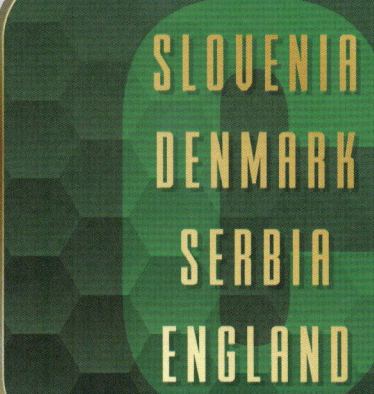

SLOVENIA
DENMARK
SERBIA
ENGLAND

SLOVENIA

FIFA WORLD RANKING 55
Colours: First:
All white
Colours: Second:
All blue
Coach:
Matjaž Kek
Captain:
Jan Oblak
Best European Championship:
Group stage (2000)

Benjamin Sesko (centre - hidden) and his Slovenia teammates celebrate after he scored their opener in a 2-0 victory against Finland in qualifying

Slovenia are back! That was the cry after their defeat of Kazakhstan in front of a record home crowd earned them second place in their qualifying group. Euro 2024 is their first major tournament since 2000 and is the culmination of improving performances under coach Matjaž Kek in the last few years.

Kek led Slovenia to the 2010 World Cup finals in his first spell in charge and was re-appointed in 2018. After failing to qualify for Euro 2020, he guided the team to a record eight-game unbeaten run and promotion in the Nations League. Despite failure to qualify for the 2022 World Cup finals, they recorded a memorable victory over Croatia and went into the Euro 2024 qualification games with confidence. Wins against Finland and Kazakhstan, and a draw with Denmark, proved enough to send them to Germany.

Slovenia's best players are positioned at either end of the pitch. In goal, they have Atlético Madrid's Jan Oblak, still only 31 years old, he is ranked among the top ten keepers in the world. Less famous but even taller, and just as integral to their qualification, is Slovenia's striker Benjamin Šeško. The forward netted five goals in nine qualifiers and has continued to impress for RB Leipzig. The other principal members of the team mostly play in Italy and Greece, including Jaka Bijol and Sandi Lovrić of Udinese, and Benjamin Verbič from Panathinaikos, and Miha Zajc of Turkish side Fenerbahçe. Slovenia's hope of progressing from the group are slight, but they will be well organised and hopeful of springing a surprise.

STAR PLAYER

BENJAMIN ŠEŠKO

At six foot, four inches (193 cm) tall the RB Leipzig striker is supremely dominant in the air, but he is also quick, agile, full of tricks and an ambush just waiting to happen for a complacent defence.

SLOVENIA - DENMARK — 41

DENMARK 🇩🇰

FIFA WORLD RANKING 21
Colours: First: Red shirts, white shorts
Colours: Second: White shirts, red shorts
Coach: Kasper Hjulmand
Captain: Simon Kjær
Best European Championship: Champions (1992)

Danish players mob Robert Skov after he scores Denmark's second goal in a crucial 3-1 victory over Kazakhstan in qualifying

Two past European Championships will feature prominently in Danish minds in Germany. Their 1992 triumph as late-entrants shocked the continent and continues to inspire the team. Then there is the 2020 tournament, where the Danes still feel aggrieved at the soft penalty that gave England an extra-time semi-final victory. They will be keen to take the opportunity for revenge in 2024.

After a 2022 World Cup in which Denmark failed to impress or progress, coach Kasper Hjulmand took them to the top of their qualifying group. A seemingly smooth ride with seven wins from ten games was interspersed with a defeat to Kazakhstan and some last-minute reprieves, but Denmark emerged feeling confident with a settled nucleus of players and at least one emerging star.

By June, goalkeeper Kasper Schmeichel, now at Anderlect, should have joined his father on a hundred caps. He is one of a group of senior players favoured by Hjulmand, including defenders Andreas Christensen of Barcelona and captain Simon Kjær who plays at Milan, and as well as midfielders in Tottenham's Pierre-Emile Højbjerg, Anderlect's Thomas Delaney and Manchester United's Christian Eriksen, who is still capable of turning a match.

With a strong centre, Denmark's overlapping full-backs (look out for Atalanta's Joakim Maehle and FC Copenhagen wonderkid Elias Jelert) and inverted wingers, like Brentford's Mikkel Damsgaard, provide attacking options. However, it is the form of Rasmus Hojlund which is key. Top scorer in their qualifying group with seven goals, if he sparks Denmark might settle a grudge and ignite that red and white dynamite.

STAR PLAYER

RASMUS HOJLUND

Despite some struggles in his first season with Manchester United, the Copenhagen-born 21-year-old has speed, strength and a definite eye for goal, and he remains Denmark's lethal attacking threat.

GROUP C

SERBIA

FIFA WORLD RANKING 32
Colours: First:
All red
Colours: Second:
All white
Coach:
Dragan Stojković
Captain:
Dušan Tadić
Best European Championship:
Quarter-Final
(2000 – As Former Yugoslavia)

Strahinja Pavlovic (No. 2) celebrates, with Sasa Lukic (No. 22) after equalising for Serbia in their qualifier against Hungary. Serbia lost the match 2-1

Serbia go into their first Euros for 24 years, and their first ever as an independent country, as one of the most unpredictable teams in the tournament. They have an experienced coach and top-rated players, and won promotion from a tough Nations League group in 2022. Yet, a draw with Cameroon earned them their only point in a disappointing World Cup finals and they made heavy going of an easy-looking Euro 2024 qualifying group.

Coach Dragan Stojković is a footballing legend in Serbia, but patience is running thin after his side continues to leak goals. He has tried a four- and a three-man defence with Nikola Milenković of Fiorentina, Werder Bremen's Miloš Veljković, the mainstays, but it hasn't been very effective and the side conceded ten goals in their last five qualifiers. However, he also has the option to add the impressive RB Salzburg centre-back Strahinja Pavlovic into the mix.

Fortunately they have a potent attacking threat in Aleksandar Mitrović, the nation's all-time record goalscorer, who has continued to find the net since his move from Fulham to Al Hilal in Saudi Arabia. He is backed by Juventus' impressive young striker Dušan Vlahović. The midfield is full of attacking promise, too. Former Lazio star Sergej Milinkovic-Savic, also now at Al Hilal, is still one of the world's best box-to-box players, while they also boast Juventus winger Filip Kostić and the experienced Dušan Tadić, who now plays at Fenerbahçe.

Serbia present an intriguing prospect in Germany. Although they face a tough challenge to finish in the group's top two, it might only take one good performance and they certainly have the attacking potential to achieve that.

ONE TO WATCH
STRAHINJA PAVLOVIC

The imposing defender's displays as centre-back for RB Salzburg have drawn the attention of Europe's super-clubs and many eyes will be on the 23-year-old in Germany, but he is unlikely to let that rattle him.

SERBIA - ENGLAND — 43

ENGLAND 🏴󠁧󠁢󠁥󠁮󠁧󠁿

Phil Foden helps Jude Bellingham (No. 10) celebrate after Marcus Rashford (not pictured) scored England's second goal against Italy at Wembley in October 2023

FIFA WORLD RANKING 3
Colours: First:
White shirts, blue shorts
Colours: Second:
All red
Coach:
Gareth Southgate
Captain:
Harry Kane
Best European Championship:
Runners-Up (2020)

England seem to have everything they need to become European Champions: a coach comfortable with his tactics, a settled team and a whole squad of top-level players. They waltzed through the qualifying competition with home and away victories over Italy helping book a place in Germany with two games to spare, and it is no wonder they are among the favourites to win the tournament.

Barring injury or tinkering with formations, much of the England team sheet can be filled in already. They have unmistakably world-class players in captain and leading goalscorer Harry Kane, now at Bayern Munich, and Real Madrid's Jude Bellingham, whose emergence as a deadly attacking midfielder has come at exactly the right time. Jordan Pickford of Everton has made the number one spot his own for some time, Newcastle's Kieran Trippier adds a dead-ball expertise to his defensive capabilities, from Arsenal come winger Bukayo Saka and midfield ball-winner Declan Rice, while Manchester City provide key defenders in John Stones, still the team's centre-back stalwart, and Kyle Walker, whose pace is priceless in attack and defence.

Is that enough for Southgate to produce a team that finally gets over the line? There are still doubts over who partners Stones in central defence and whether Tottenham Hotspur's James Maddison, Manchester City's Phil Foden or Jack Grealish, or Liverpool's Alexander-Arnold can provide the midfield creativity that is sometimes lacking in England sides. On paper they are strong, though, and it will probably come down to a piece of skill or slice of luck in that crucial match.

STAR PLAYER

JUDE BELLINGHAM

The rapid development of the 21-year-old into a world-class midfielder who is capable of making driving runs from deep, assists and goals has given England an exciting new attacking impetus.

GROUP D

France hope to go all the way to the final, but first face an improving Netherlands, an unpredictable Austrian team and Poland energised by their play-off victory.

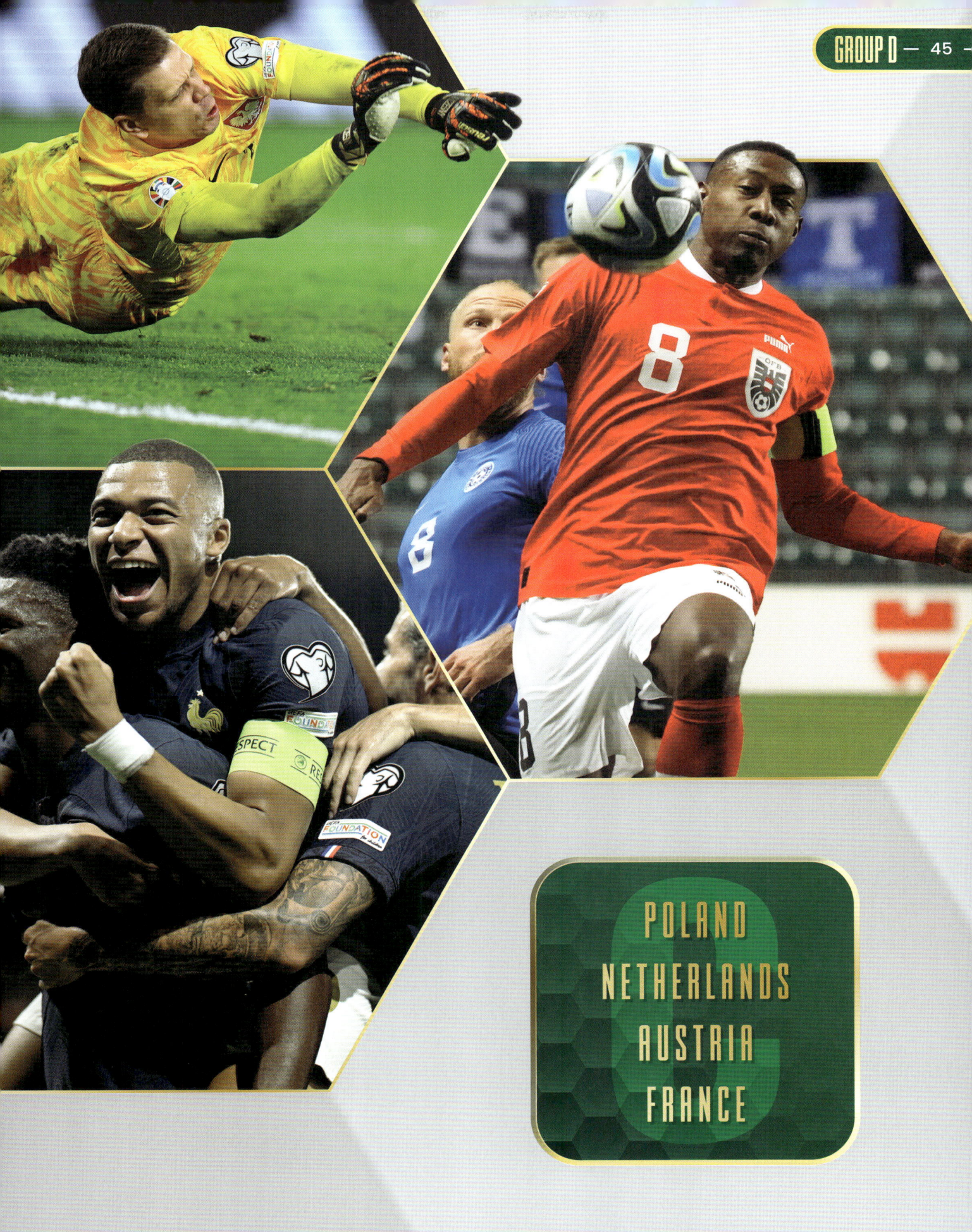

GROUP D — 45

POLAND
NETHERLANDS
AUSTRIA
FRANCE

GROUP D

POLAND

FIFA WORLD RANKING 30
Colours: First:
White shirts, red shorts
Colours: Second:
Red shirts, white shorts
Coach:
Michał Probierz
Captain:
Robert Lewandowski
Best European Championship:
Quarter-Final (2016)

Poland's Wojciech Szczęsny saves final penalty kick during the UEFA EURO 2024 Play-offs semi-final against Wales at Cardiff City Stadium on March 26, 2024

Despite reaching the Round of 16 at the 2022 World Cup where they were defeated by France, Poland have often struggled to find form in the Nations League or the qualifiers which saw embarrassing defeats to Albania and Moldova. Optimism, however, can be found in recent results and the presence of one of the world's best strikers.

The team's upturn has coincided with the appointment of coach Michał Probierz, who arrived in October 2023 and has guided them through the second half of qualifying where they remained unbeaten. Probierz can take credit for building a good team spirit and bringing defensive stability to Poland's performances. His priority is safety with three central midfielders sitting back and attacks coming from the flanks or created by the strikers dropping back.

Probierz can rely on Juventus goalkeeper Wojciech Szczęsny and a defence that includes Arsenal's Jakub Kiwior and Jan Badenek of Southampton. Bartosz Slisz (Atalanta) and Piotr Zieliński (Napoli) are key holding midfielders, while of the wing-backs Przemysław Frankowski (Lens) is an adept crosser and Nicola Zalewski (Roma) is speedy and full of tricks. The goalscoring legend Robert Lewandowski (Barcelona) is usually paired with Karol Świderski (Hellas Verona) as strikers required to make optimum use of scant chances.

Poland's reward for winning the penalty shoot-out against Wales in their qualifying play-off is a place in one of the toughest Euro 2024 groups. They will be hard to beat and might have been fancied to progress from an easier group, but Euro 2024 will be Lewandowski's swan song and he may still have a say in how it plays out.

STAR PLAYER

ROBERT LEWANDOWSKI

A move to Barcelona hasn't dimmed Lewandowski's potency as a goal-maker and scorer. Even in the twilight of his career he is still a lethal goal threat.

Wout Weghorst (No. 9) celebrates with Frenkie de Jong having put the Netherlands 3-0 up against Greece in their qualifying tie

NETHERLANDS

FIFA WORLD RANKING 6
Colours: First:
All orange
Colours: Second:
All blue
Coach:
Ronald Koeman
Captain:
Virgil Van Dijk
Best European Championship:
Champions (1988)

The Netherlands' qualifying campaign – and Ronald Koeman's first game back in charge of the Oranje – began with a 4-0 thrashing at the hands of France. It got no better when the country hosted the Nations League finals and were defeated by Croatia and Italy. With numerous players missing through injury, many feared they would miss out on qualification for Euro 2024, but they won every game (bar another defeat by France) and were safe in second place.

Koeman has had little chance to build a steady team and to implement his favoured line-up and tactics. What he does have is a squad that is deep in quality, especially at the back, where he is spoiled for choice. As well as Inter's Stefan de Vrij, Matthijs De Ligt of Bayern Munich, Liverpool's Virgil van Dijk and Feyenoord's Quilindschy Hartman, he can call on Sven Botman from Newcastle, Inter's Denzel Dumfries, Manchester City's Nathan Aké, Tottenham's Micky van de Ven, Daley Blind of Girona or even Ajax's new star, 18-year-old Jorrel Hato.

Various names have been put forward to partner Barcelona's Frenkie de Jong in the centre of midfield with Milan's Tijjani Reijnders the favourite candidate or possible Atalanta's Teun Koopmeiners. The lack of firepower up front may be a bigger issue.

The tall Wout Weghorst from Hoffenheim has played alongside Memphis Depay of Atlético Madrid, Steven Bergwijn of Ajax and Liverpool's Cody Gakpo, but there is pressure for 21-year-old Bryan Brobbey, who has had a great season with Ajax, to be called up.

Netherlands can expect to progress from the group and Koeman may well work his magic and produce a team that can challenge for the title. Regardless, another encounter with France is undeniably mouth watering.

STAR PLAYER

FRENKIE DE JONG

The perfect central midfielder, he breaks up opposition moves and creates attacks. Back to his best after injury, Frenkie will be hoping to make the Oranje tick in Germany.

AUSTRIA

FIFA WORLD RANKING 25

Colours: First:
All red
Colours: Second:
White shirts, black shorts
Coach:
Ralf Rangnick
Captain:
David Alaba
Best European Championship:
Round Of 16 (2020)

Austria's David Alaba (No. 8), watched by Marco Sabitzer (No. 9), in action against Estonia in November 2023

Austria had an image problem. Seen as a team of uninspiring players playing dull football, even successes like reaching the round of 16 in Euro 2020 and going out after a 2-1 defeat in extra-time had failed to raise pulses. Then came Ralf Rangnick. Off the back of a disappointing time as interim coach at Manchester United, he took over in June 2022. Out went the defensive, low-confidence football and in came a high-press, risk-taking, attacking game. And it seems to have worked.

An incredible 3-0 thrashing of Croatia marked the start of Rangnick's reign, but it wasn't plain sailing. Despite relegation in the Nations League after defeats by France, Denmark and Croatia in the return match, the fans and players kept faith. This was justified when they waltzed through Euro 2024 qualification with just one narrow defeat to group winners Belgium and recorded impressive victories home and away over Sweden.

Rangnick's high-energy style makes his formations fluid, but he has senior players from Europe's top leagues who have bought into the plan. First and foremost, Real Madrid defender and team captain, David Alaba, but also centre-back Stefan Posch from Bologna, midfielders Marcel Sabitzer of Dortmund, Xaver Schlager and Christoph Baumgartner, both from RB Leipzig, and Konrad Laimer of Bayern Munich as well as Inter Milan's veteran goalscorer Marko Arnautović.

The team's new attitude has caught the public imagination, which is further encouraged by the inclusion of home-based players with RB Salzburg's Alexander Schlager, now the first-choice keeper, and young midfielders Matthias Seidl of Rapid Wien and Alex Prass of Sturm Graz getting game time. Despite Rangnick's bold approach, Austria may not progress in the tournament, but it will be fun watching them try.

STAR PLAYER

DAVID ALABA

Nine times Austrian Footballer of the Year and three time Champions League winner, at 31 years old Alaba is still classy, effective and one of the world's best left-backs.

FRANCE

Aurélien Tchouaméni (r) celebrates his goal with Kylian Mbappé (top) and Theo Hernández (l) of France during their 2-0 qualifier victory over Republic of Ireland at Parc des Princes

FIFA WORLD RANKING 2
Colours: First: Dark blue shirts, white shorts
Colours: Second: White shirts, light blue shorts
Coach: Didier Deschamps
Captain: Kylian Mbappé
Best European Championship: Champions (1984, 2000)

Plus ça change… Since their 2022 World Cup final penalty shoot-out defeat to Argentina, major players Hugo Lloris, Raphael Varane and Karim Benzema may have retired, but Didier Deschamps, coach since 2012, has signed up for three-and-a-half more years and his team have continued to look just as formidable. As Argentina, Croatia, Denmark and even Germany have proved over the past two years, France are beatable, but Les Bleus will take some stopping in Germany.

Just a draw with Greece prevented France from completing a perfect qualification campaign, as they won seven of eight, scored 29 goals (including a record 14 against Gibraltar) and conceded just three. Wherever you look in the squad there is quality; from Arsenal's 22-year-old defender William Saliba, who isn't even a guaranteed start, to 37-year-old Olivier Giroud, now at AC Milan and the nation's greatest ever goalscorer.

Milan goalkeeper Mike Maignan has stepped seamlessly into Lloris's boots, while in defence they can turn to Bayern Munich's Dayot Upamecano and Benjamin Pavard, Barcelona's Jules Koundé, the Hernández brothers Lucas of PSG and Théo of Milan, both world-class full-backs and Liverpool's Ibrahima Konaté. In midfield, Real Madrid's Aurélien Tchouaméni plays the holding role along with Adrien Rabiot of Juventus. Meanwhile, 32-year-old Antoine Griezmann continues to pull the strings. And, if having one of the world's greatest strikers in Kylian Mbappé is not enough, his PSG teammates Ousmane Dembélé and Randal Kolo Muani are standing by.

Deschamps's embarrassment of riches continues with the emerging generation. Real Madrid's outstanding defensive midfielder Eduardo Camavinga is just 21, while 18-year-old midfielder Warren Zaïre-Emery steals the limelight. Already a regular for PSG, he is France's next wonderboy, their youngest debutant and scorer for over a century.

STAR PLAYER

KYLIAN MBAPPE

A Golden Ball winner and hat-trick hero of the final in the 2022 World Cup, Mbappé's speed, control and goalscoring acumen is sure to dazzle once more in Germany.

GROUP E

Belgium looked to have lucked out with an easy group draw, but can take nothing for granted. Meanwhile, the battle for second or even a well-placed third could be fierce...

GROUP E — 51

BELGIUM
SLOVAKIA
ROMANIA
UKRAINE

BELGIUM

FIFA WORLD RANKING 4

Colours: First:
Red shirts, black shorts

Colours: Second:
All white

Coach:
Domenico Tedesco

Captain:
Kevin De Bruyne

Best European Championship:
Semi-Final (2020)

Belgium's Romelu Lukaku celebrates with Jérémy Doku after scoring the opening goal during the Euro 2024 qualifying match against Azerbaijan at the King Baudouin Stadium in November 2023

The Red Devils's so-called "golden generation" are slowly leaving the stage having failed to achieve the glory their talent promised. With them, after exiting meekly in the Euro 2020 and 2022 World Cup finals, went coach Roberto Martinez. In came Italian and former RB Leipzig coach Domenico Tedesco and a new era was born.

The new coach has remained unbeaten throughout his first year in charge. The team sailed unbeaten through the qualifications, winning six and drawing two games, scoring 22 goals along the way. They also recorded a benchmark victory over Euro hosts Germany in a friendly in Cologne. With world class players in goalkeeper Thibaut Courtois and midfielder Kevin de Bryune both missing a huge chunk of the season, and other senior players retiring, Tedesco turned to youth with Premier League midfielders in Chelsea's Romeo Lavia and Everton's Amadou Onana, as well as PSV forward Johan Bakayoko, Manchester City winger Jérémy Doku and Rennes defender Arthur Theate all justifying his faith.

Belgium can still rely on their leading appearance-maker Jan Vertonghen, now at Anderlecht, and their greatest-ever scorer in Romelu Lukaku, currently at Roma, but across the pitch they are looking for senior players to step up. Going forward, there is a pool of exciting players, including Aston Villa's Youri Tielemans, Arsenal's Leandro Trossard and Bologna's Alexis Saelemaekers, and established strikers in Michy Batshuayi of Fenebache and Yannick Carrasco of Al Shabab. However, doubts remain over the strength of the back four – often Vertonghen and Theate with Fulham's Timothy Castagne and Leicester City's Wout Faes.

The pressure is off Belgium. With captain Kevin De Bruyne back from injury and in form, and enough of the young guns firing, they could still prove to be dangerous outsiders.

ONE TO WATCH

JÉRÉMY DOKU

The 22-year-old winger has had a sparkling debut season for Manchester City. His ball control has bamboozled defenders and left spectators open-mouthed. Spectators can look forward to more of that in Germany.

SLOVAKIA

Slovakia's Stanislav Lobotka (No. 22) celebrates with teammates after scoring his team's second goal during the Euro 2024 qualifying match against Portugal at Estádio do Dragão in October 2023

FIFA WORLD RANKING 48
Colours: First:
All blue
Colours: Second:
All white with blue sleeves
Coach:
Francesco Calzona
Captain:
Milan Škriniar
Best European Championship:
Round Of 16 (2016)

Ever since the number of teams was increased from 16 to 24 in 2016, Slovakia have qualified for successive European Championship finals. That says something about their place in the football firmament. They qualified for Euro 2024, suffering just two close defeats to Portugal, but did exactly enough in gaining enough points from lower ranked teams to finish as runners-up.

Slovakia go to Germany with a big Marek Hamšík-sized hole in their squad. The national legend, leading appearance-maker and leading scorer, retired in 2022 and, despite making a comeback to help the team in the qualifiers, is only at the finals as part of the coaching staff. However, they do have top-class players in Newcastle United goalkeeper Martin Dúbravka, PSG centre-back Milan Škriniar and Napoli midfielder Stanislav Lobotka.

Coach Calzona likes his team to defend with a high line and press opponents in their own half, relying on rapid counter-attacks. Much will depend on the stars of the team being ably supported by those playing in Europe's top leagues, including veteran right-back Hertha Berlin's Peter Pekarík, Feyenoord centre-back Dávid Hancko, playmaker Ondrej Duda of Hellas Verona and a forward line spearheaded by Boavista's Róbert Boženík.

Slovakia have never shone at the Euros, but have always delivered a surprise, beating Poland in 2016 and defeating Russia in 2020. This time round their ambitions should be set higher. Belgium aside, they are as good as any team in this group, so making the knock-out stage should be achievable. Perhaps they can save the shock result for then?

STAR PLAYER

STANISLAV LOBOTKA

He was at the heart of Napoli's 2023 Serie A-winning team, and Lobotka's tackling and vision in central midfield are equally important to his nation's efforts and potential success.

ROMANIA

FIFA WORLD RANKING 45
Colours: First:
Yellow shirts, white shorts
Colours: Second:
All white
Coach:
Edward Iordănescu
Captain:
Nicolae Stanciu
Best European Championship:
Quarter-Final (2000)

Radu Dragusin (No. 3), Denis Alibec (No. 7) and Nicolae Stanciu (No. 10) of Romania celebrate after their 1-0 defeat of Switzerland ensures they top qualifying Group I

After an eight-year wait, Romania finally qualified for a major finals, topping a group that included the much higher-ranked Switzerland. The team is coached by Edward Iordănescu, son of former national team coach Anghel, who led Romania in their glory years of the 1990s. This team lacks the style of that famous line-up, which included Gheorghe Hagi, Ilie Dumitrescu and Florin Răducioiu, but they are a well-drilled and compact unit. They were undefeated in qualification with six wins and four draws, and conceded only five goals in ten matches.

Although a team with few internationally known names, Romania boast stand-out players in captain Nicolae Stanciu, an attacking midfielder who has won league titles in Romania, Czech Republic and China, and now plays in Saudi Arabia; Empoli midfielder Răzvan Marin; and Genoa forward George Pușcaș. Others who may make a name for themselves in Germany include Tottenham defender Radu Drăgușin; Alaves midfielder Ianis Hagi (son of the aforementioned Gheorghe Hagi, Romania's greatest ever player); Darius Olaru, captain of leading Romanian team FCSB (formerly Steau Bucharest); and Parma winger Valentin Mihăilă.

A resurgent team like Romania, who climbed nine places in the FIFA rankings over 2023, are always a danger. Their defence will be difficult to break down and they have shown they can launch incisive attacks. Their main weaknesses are that they don't really have a player of match-winning quality and their lack of experience against top teams in major finals. Nevertheless, with organisation and togetherness they are well capable of progressing from this group.

ONE TO WATCH

RADU DRĂGUȘIN

The 22-year-old central defender signed for Tottenham Hotspur in January 2024. He is a commanding figure at the back, tall and strong and comfortable in possession

UKRAINE

FIFA WORLD RANKING 24

Colours: First: All yellow, blue trim
Colours: Second: All blue, yellow trim
Coach: Serhiy Rebrov
Captain: Andriy Yarmolenko
Best European Championship: Quarter-Final (2020)

Mykhailo Mudryk of Ukraine battling Giovanni Di Lorenzo of Italy during the Group C UEFA EURO 2024 European Qualifiers match between Ukraine and Italy at BayArena on November 20, 2023

With their country ravaged by war and having to play their home matches in other nations, Ukraine lost just twice in qualifying and were desperately unlucky to be edged into the play-offs on head-to-head results by Italy. In both the play-off ties, against Bosnia and Herzegovina and Iceland, they found themselves a goal down until late in the game. They showed incredible passion and spirit to force a victory – qualities that will serve them well in Germany.

Coach Serhiy Rebrov, a Ukrainian footballing legend, has built a team around more than passion. They are a possession-based team and like to control the flanks with many of their attacking moves beginning from wide positions. Rebrov is not afraid to make mid-game tactical changes and substitutions, and has shown he believes none of his players are indispensable.

Fortunately, he has a squad of top league players. With a choice of excellent keepers, it is Andriy Lunin, Courtois' understudy at Real Madrid, who is currently favoured. Midfield is Ukraine's engine and creative force. It includes wingers in Chelsea's Mykhailo Mudryk and Oleksiy Gutsulyak of Dnipro, as well as promising Dynamo Kyiv star Volodymyr Brazhko, the experienced Oleksandr Zinchenko (Arsenal) and Andriy Yarmolenko now at Dynamo. Up front, Girona's Viktor Tsyhankov has been a handful in qualifiers and is well supported by Valencia's Roman Yaremchuk and Girona's Artem Dovbyk.

Ukraine will have great public support in Germany and have shown they have the spirit and ability to make a memorable impression on the tournament if results fall their way.

ONE TO WATCH

MYKHAILO MUDRYK

The expensive 23-year-old had a difficult first season at Chelsea, but glimpses of brilliant wing play have shown he has much more to offer.

GROUP F

Portugal, the best team in qualifying, are clear favourites in the group, leaving a three-way battle between Turkey, Czech Republic and Georgia that could go to the wire.

TURKEY 🇹🇷

FIFA WORLD RANKING 35
Colours: First:
All white
Colours: Second:
All red
Coach:
Vincenzo Montella
Captain:
Hakan Çalhanoğlu
Best European Championship:
Semi-Final (2008)

Turkey players celebrate after Baris Yilmaz (no. 11) put Turkey ahead against Croatia in qualifying. Turkey won the match 1-0

September 2023. Having failed to qualify for the 2022 World Cup, Turkey needed a late equaliser to salvage a point at home to Armenia. Their second place in the Euro 2024 qualifying group looked precarious and, after a friendly defeat by Japan, Stefan Kunz was replaced as coach by Vincenzo Montella.

The transformation was immediate. The Italian Montella, who has a reputation for being tactically astute, combined youth and experience, and utilised his skilful attacking players. A magnificent win in Croatia and a draw in Wales enabled the Turks to top the group, with a friendly victory over Germany adding to the new-found momentum.

Montella's team builds from a secure back four, with highly rated full-backs in Fenerbahçe's Ferdi Kadioglu and Valencia's Cenk Özkacar. The attacking thrust in midfield falls to Inter Milan star Hakan Çalhanoğlu, while alongside him are Borussia Dortmund's defensive midfielder Salih Özcan, Benfica's exciting box-to-box dynamo Orkun Kökçü, and wingers Kerem Akturkoglu of Galatasaray and Cengiz Ünder, also of Fenerbahçe.

Montella has not been scared to look to emerging talent, too. Galatasaray's 24-year-old forward Bariş Alper Yilmaz has been employed as a lone striker; Kenan Yildiz, a 19-year-old attacking midfielder and Juventus's youngest ever goalscorer, is gaining international experience; and, at the same age, left-sided midfielder Arda Güler is being heralded as Real Madrid's latest rising star.

Turkey were tipped by many to be dark horses at Euro 2020, yet went on to lose all three group games, so many pundits are being cautious this time. However, their impressive form since Montella took charge has certainly given cause for optimism.

STAR PLAYER:
HAKAN ÇALHANOĞLU

One of Europe's best midfielders, Çalhanoğlu has been applauded when he plays in a deep-lying role for Inter, but Turkey have employed him as an equally effective No.10.

Georgia's players celebrate after winning the UEFA EURO 2024 qualifying play-off final against Greece in Tbilisi on March 26, 2024

GEORGIA

FIFA WORLD RANKING 77
Colours: First:
All white, red trim
Colours: Second:
All black, red trim
Coach:
Willy Sagnol
Captain:
Guram Kashai
Best European Championship:
First-Time Qualifiers

Bitter disappointment at missing out on Euro 2020 in the qualification play-off finals was wiped out in March 2024 as 10-men Georgia earned a historic first major tournament place after a shoot-out triumph over Greece in Tbilisi. Since becoming coach in 2012, former France international defender, Willy Sagnol, has overseen a clear improvement in results. Georgia won promotion in the Nations League and registered draws with Norway and Scotland in their Euro qualifiers.

Sagnol has been blessed with a formidable crop of young players. He has given them confidence and allowed them to take risks. Under his guidance they have developed a defensive solidity with considerable attacking flair. A quick transition between the two is essential to their game and, if successful, could worry higher ranked teams.

Georgia have a number of highly rated players in their early-20s, such as Valencia goalkeeper Giorgi Mamardashvili, Torino centre-back Saba Sazonov, right-back Giorgi Gocholeishvili of Shakhtar Donetsk and Watford winger, Giorgi Chakvetadze. The focus, though, is on the attacking threat of Napoli's golden boy Khvicha Kvaratskhelia and Metz forward Georges Mikautadze, France's Ligue 2 top scorer in 2022-23.

They are not without experience, though. Captain Guram Kashai, a Slovan Bratislava defender, has over 100 caps, while his club teammate, midfielder Jaba Kankava, came out of retirement for the qualifiers and might be persuaded to stay for the tournament.

Georgia are the only debutante nation in Germany. In Kvaratskhelia, they have a match-winner and must believe they have a chance of snatching second place in an open group.

STAR PLAYER

KHVICHA KVARATSKHELIA

At Napoli, they call their wing wizard 'Kvaradona'. Still only 23, he was instrumental in their 2022-23 Serie A triumph and was the 2023 Champions League Young Player of the Season.

PORTUGAL

FIFA WORLD RANKING 7
Colours: First:
Red shirts, green shorts
Colours: Second:
All white
Coach:
Roberto Martínez
Captain:
Cristiano Ronaldo
Best European Championship:
Champions (2016)

Cristiano Ronaldo celebrates his strike for Portugal against Liechtenstein in qualifying in 2023. It was his 41st goal in Euro qualifying rounds, an all-time record

The winners of the 2016 Euros and the inaugural Nations League final in 2019 hit the bumpers in the 2020 Euros and 2022 World Cup, and it has taken Roberto Martínez, appointed coach in January 2023, to rebuild the side. Fortunately, he has world-class stars to help, including Manchester City's Rúben Dias and Bernardo Silva, Manchester United's Bruno Fernandes and an irrepressible 39-year-old Cristiano Ronaldo.

There were doubts over Ronaldo's international future following Portugal's disappointing 2022 World Cup, but despite the star decamping to play in Saudi, Martínez included him in his squad. It was a great decision. Portugal had an easy group on paper with only Bosnia and Herzegovina, Iceland and Slovakia to worry them. Nevertheless, they won every one of their matches, including a Portuguese record 9-0 victory over Luxembourg, and conceded in just one game, against Slovakia.

There is quality right across the team. The brilliant Porto goalkeeper Diogo Costa caps a strong defensive unit that includes Dias, his former Manchester City teammate João Cancelo, now at Barcelona, PSG's Danilo and Sporting's Gonçalo Inácio, who is already in the sights of Europe's richest clubs. In midfield they boast the creative qualities of Fernandes and Silva alongside emerging stars João Neves of Benfica and Vitinha from PSG. Ronaldo continues to be a colossus upfront, but Martínez can also call on Barcelona's João Félix, PSG's Gonçalo Ramos and AC Milan's Rafael Leão.

Could their kind qualification draw have exaggerated Portugal's chances? With such quality running all the way through the squad, Portugal have every reason to believe they can beat any team in the tournament and it will be intriguing to see how they fare against top opposition.

ONE TO WATCH

DIOGO COSTA

The Porto keeper could well be on his way to one of Europe's top clubs by the time the World Cup has finished. Now 24 years old, he has long been viewed as a future superstar and is fulfilling his potential.

CZECH REPUBLIC

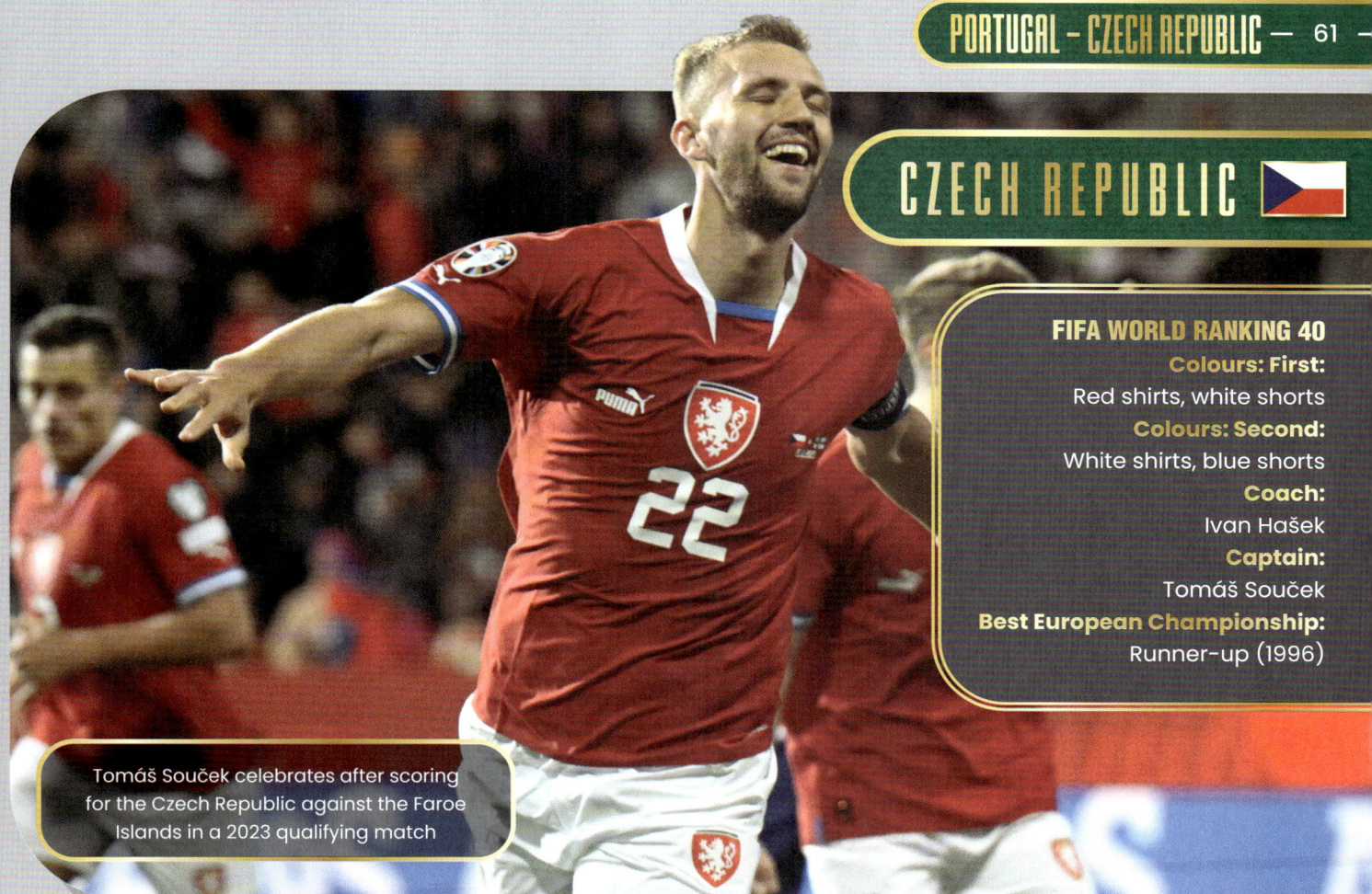

Tomáš Souček celebrates after scoring for the Czech Republic against the Faroe Islands in a 2023 qualifying match

FIFA WORLD RANKING 40
Colours: First:
Red shirts, white shorts
Colours: Second:
White shirts, blue shorts
Coach:
Ivan Hašek
Captain:
Tomáš Souček
Best European Championship:
Runner-up (1996)

A 3-0 victory over Moldova in their final qualifying match secured Czech Republic a place in their eighth successive Euros after finishing second to Albania. The campaign was fraught, with the Czech team in danger of missing out on automatic qualification throughout. It ended in chaos as well, with three players sent home on the eve of the last match and coach Jaroslav Silhavy announcing his resignation soon after sealing a spot in Germany.

Euro 2020 saw Czech Republic emerge as one of the surprise packages of the tournament. They reached the quarter-finals by way of a shock 2-0 defeat of Netherlands, where they suffered a close defeat by Denmark. The hero of that team was Patrik Schick, but his absence through injury throughout Euro 2024 qualification was a major issue for the Czechs. The 28-year old's 2024 return to fitness and goalscoring form for Bayer Leverkusen will raise spirits among fans.

The team contain few other stars with players from Slavia and Sparta Prague forming the bulk of the squad. They can look to West Ham United teammates midfielder Tomáš Souček and full-back Vladimír Coufal, Fiorentina's attacking midfielder Antonín Barák and Bundesliga stars in rampaging wing-back Pavel Kaderabek of Hoffenheim, midfield anchor Alex Král from Union Berlin and Bayer Leverkusen's exciting young forward Adam Hložek.

The chances of this Czech team emulating their 2020 success rests heavily on the shoulders of the new coach Ivan Hašek, but before a ball is kicked, they are looking pretty slim.

STAR PLAYER

PATRIK SCHICK

Scorer of a remarkable strike from the halfway line against Scotland and equal top marksman in the 2020 tournament, can Schick repeat his heroics in Germany? Time will tell.

THE HISTORY OF THE EUROPEAN CHAMPIONSHIP

The European Championship has come a long way since 1960, when 17 nations competed for places at the four-team finals in France. There were 53 nations competing for the 23 available places (hosts Germany qualified automatically) at the 2024 finals. Germany (including West Germany) are the most successful nation. They have made the final six times and, along with Spain, have won it three times, with France and Italy both lifting the coveted trophy twice. Here are the fascinating stories of those tournaments.

THE HISTORY OF THE EUROPEAN CHAMPIONSHIP — 63

THE HISTORY OF THE EUROPEAN CHAMPIONSHIP

EUROPEAN NATIONS' CUP 1960

FRANCE

Here's a quiz question for you: at which major international football tournament were only three, rather than the more usual four, quarter-finals played? The answer? It was the first European Championship – or European Nations' Cup as it was called at the time – which took place in 1960 in France.

That inaugural competition had 17 entrants, but the initial roster didn't include England, Scotland, Wales, Northern Ireland, Belgium, the Netherlands, Switzerland, Italy or West Germany. Three years previously those countries had voted against establishing a continent-level tournament and stubbornly refused to participate.

In terms of the structure, there was a preliminary round at which the Republic of Ireland went out. In the round of 16, the teams then played home and away legs until there were eight quarter-finalists. France then beat Austria, Yugoslavia beat Portugal and Czechoslovakia beat Romania.

The Spanish were set to face the Soviet Union, but Spain were ruled by the fascist dictator Franco, who baulked at the idea of his country's team travelling to a Communist country and playing the Soviets. Spain didn't turn up for the game in front of a sell-out Moscow crowd, they were disqualified and the USSR got a pass through to the semi-finals.

France then agreed to host the mini knockout tournament consisting of two semi-finals and one final, plus the third-place playoff, in Paris. In those days international travel wasn't particularly easy, especially if you were coming from Eastern Europe as three of the four contenders were. It took the Yugoslavian team 28 hours on a train to reach the French capital and then they had to do the last kilometre on foot, carrying their own luggage, as no transport to their hotel had been arranged.

Dragan Džajić of Yugoslavia

Czech goalkeeper Viliam Schrojf thwarts a Soviet Union attack during his team's semi-final defeat in the 1960 championships

They had been drawn to play the home team in what turned out to be the match of the tournament. In a half-full Parc des Princes both sides scored after about ten minutes, but François Heutte put France ahead just before half-time and just after half-time Maryan Wisniewski made it 3-1.

Despite being racked by injuries and short on experience, the French looked in a comfortable position until Dragan Šekularac pulled one back for the Yugoslavs. Arguably France's keeper, Georges Lamia, was at fault for the goal, but France weren't deterred and headed straight for the other end where Heutte scored.

It was 4-2 with a quarter of an hour to go, but France's day suddenly took a sharp turn for the worse as Lamia let in three goals in quick succession. The first of these shots squeezed past him. He dropped the next and for the third goal the ball slipped out of his hands and was tapped in. It finished 4-5 to Yugoslavia, who were through to the final.

By contrast, the other semi-final, at Marseille's Stade Vélodrome, was fairly eventless with the USSR overcoming Czechoslovakia 3-0 through technical ability and work rate.

THE HISTORY OF THE EUROPEAN CHAMPIONSHIP

1960 FINAL: Soviet Union 2-1 Yugoslavia (a.e.t.)

If Franco hadn't interfered would Spain have made it through to the end and lifted the first European Championship trophy? We will never know, but the final itself still wasn't exempt from politics because, going back more than a decade, the Yugoslavian leader Tito had broken with Moscow and its leader, one Joseph Stalin, and, even though Stalin was dead at this point, there were noticeable residual tensions.

Yugoslavia took charge from the off and the pressure they exerted was rewarded by a goal that slid past USSR's legendary keeper Lev Yashin just before half-time. It was credited to Milan Galić, but he didn't seem to know much about it and it could have gone in off the Soviets' Igor Netto, who was marking him.

However, within minutes of the restart the USSR scored, Metreveli tapping in a loose ball. They didn't really deserve it, but it seemed to knock the stuffing out of the Yugoslavians a bit and despite a couple of Soviet chances it remained 1-1 at full-time.

It went to extra-time, but Yugoslavia's Galić missed a sitter and the stalemate continued until, with just seven minutes left, Viktor Ponedelnik's head connected with a cross from Valentin Ivanov, the Soviet national side's third-highest scorer of all time, and the USSR became the first champions of Europe.

Worthy of a brief footnote is the fact that the final was refereed by veteran English ref Arthur Ellis, who not only reffed the famous 1954 'Battle of Berne' between Hungary and Brazil (Hungary won 4-2), but in later life was also an adjudicator on the popular British TV gameshow *It's a Knockout*.

MAGIC MOMENTS
FOUNDING FATHER

The winning USSR team were presented with the first Henri Delaunay Cup, named after the Frenchman who came up with the concept of a continental competition, although sadly Delaunay died in 1958 and never saw his idea realised.

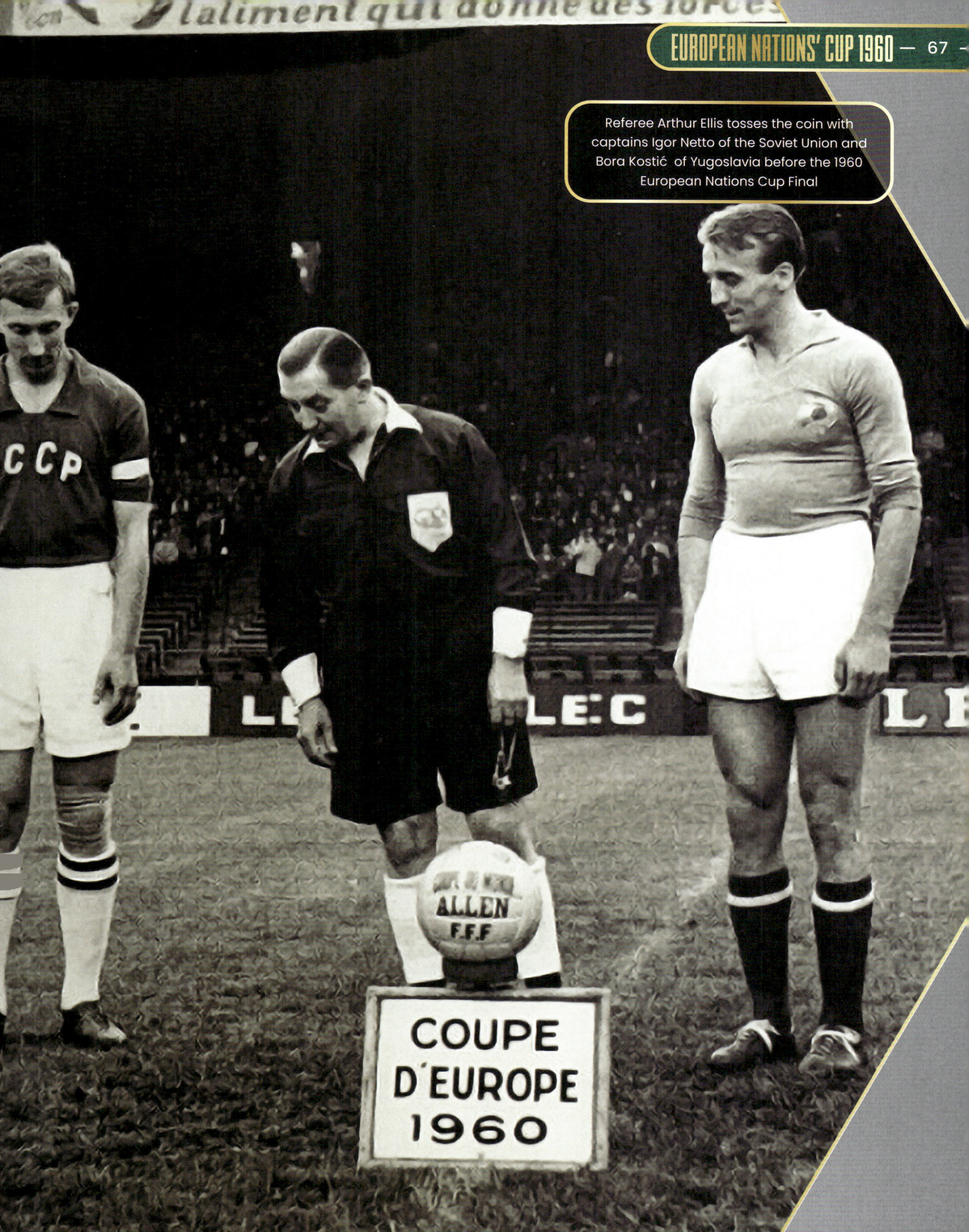

EUROPEAN NATIONS' CUP 1960 — 67

Referee Arthur Ellis tosses the coin with captains Igor Netto of the Soviet Union and Bora Kostić of Yugoslavia before the 1960 European Nations Cup Final

THE HISTORY OF THE EUROPEAN CHAMPIONSHIP

EUROPEAN NATIONS' CUP 1964

The format was essentially the same as the previous edition, but in 1964 a total of 29 teams entered the European Nations' Cup, as it was still called, including England and Italy, but not West Germany, and Greece, who pulled out rather than face Albania (for political rather than footballing reasons).

Tiny Luxembourg were the surprise success of the two-leg qualifying rounds, first beating the Netherlands and then drawing twice with Denmark. That forced a replay, which unfortunately they lost, so it was the Danes who progressed to join previous champions the Soviet Union, Hungary and Spain in the last four. The venues for the final matches were decided once the teams were known and on this occasion Spain was chosen.

Camp Nou was the venue for what turned out to be a rather unequal battle between Denmark and the USSR. In theory the competition was strictly all-amateur and indeed the Danes had lost several players from its earlier stages because they had turned professional. However, the Russians were tough, efficient and experienced, and within 20 minutes they were 1-0 up, thanks to a strike from Valery Voronin.

Five minutes before the whistle went for half-time Viktor Ponedelnik got the second, beating Danish keeper Leif Nielsen, who had only recently stepped up to senior level, easily. The game was essentially over, but six minutes from the end Valentin Ivanov stylishly sealed the deal to make it 3-0. The USSR were in the final again and potentially on their way to a second successive trophy.

In the early stages of the competition the hosts had been missing Luis Suárez, one of the greatest Spanish players of all time, but fortunately for them the elegant midfielder was available for Spain's semi-final against Hungary at the Bernabéu in Madrid. He dominated the first half and ten minutes before the break his cross into the box found Chus Pereda's head and the ball hit the top corner of the net. Hungarian keeper Antal Szentmihályi could only stand and watch, and Spain went 1-0 up.

In the second half Suárez seemed to be carrying an injury and made less of an impact, but that wasn't a big issue until Spanish keeper José Angel Iribar lost the ball and made the mistake that allowed Hungary's Ferenc Bene to equalise six minutes before full-time. That meant it went to extra-time.

Before the match all the talk had been about the Hungarians' stamina, so the Spaniards must have been nervous about whether they could keep up with the Eastern Europeans, but in truth their opponents were out of ideas and eight minutes before the end Amancio poked the ball past Szentmihályi from close quarters and the home side were through to the final, 2-1.

EUROPEAN NATIONS' CUP 1964 — 69

Valery Voronin of The Soviet Union

1964 FINAL — Spain 2-1 Soviet Union

Four years previously General Franco, the Spanish dictator, had refused to allow his national side to travel to Moscow to play the Soviet Union. Now he was present in person on home ground, in the Bernabéu, in front of over 79,000 fans, as the two teams met to settle the European Championship. Those who were there said it also felt like a clash between two political ideologies – a communist regime versus a right-wing dictatorship.

At first the game was very open, but Suárez quickly made his mark again, sending a free kick over the bar and then, after six minutes, beating a bunch of defenders before crossing again to set up Pereda once more. However, the Soviets retaliated rapidly, when, a couple of minutes later, Iribar failed to hold on to a hopeful tap-in from Galimzyan Khusainov.

It was 1-1 as the teams went in at half-time, but when they emerged again for the second half there was a fair amount of argy-bargy and somewhat lax refereeing meant that players on both sides went unpunished for some quite nasty fouls. Suárez seemed to lose his grip on the game after a kick, albeit an accidental one this time, from Russian defender – and 1964's Soviet Footballer of the Year –Voronin. However, there was very little to separate the teams until, in the 84th minute, Marcelino scored with a header and Spain were European champions.

The following day Franco held a reception for the Spanish manager José Villalonga Llorente and his squad and the press praised them to the skies. Back in Moscow, the Russian coach Konstantin Beskov was immediately sacked by Soviet premier Nikita Khrushchev, who was apparently incensed that they had lost and 'let down' their country.

MAGIC MOMENTS
UNSUNG HERO

No one remembers the name of the Spanish coach, but even before he took over as boss of the national team he had had an illustrious career, winning titles and trophies with both Real Madrid and Atletico Madrid. However, the pinnacle of José Villalonga's success was guiding Spain to their 1964 European Nations' Cup victory.

EUROPEAN NATIONS' CUP 1964 — 71

The Soviet Union captain Valentin Ivanov (r) exchanges handshakes and pennants with Spain skipper Ferran Olivella before the 1964 final

THE HISTORY OF THE EUROPEAN CHAMPIONSHIP

EUROPEAN CHAMPIONSHIP 1968

ITALY

Revolution was in the air in Europe in 1968 and there were changes to the European Nations' Cup, too, albeit fairly minimal ones. The tournament officially became the European Football Championship and instead of two-leg knockout ties, there were now eight qualifying groups. England qualified from a Home Championship group – despite Scotland inflicting their first post-World Cup defeat – and Italy responded to their 1966 embarrassment at the hands of North Korea by sailing through. However, West Germany, held to a draw in Albania, failed to advance in their first appearance in the competition. Although Netherlands also missed out, their first game, against Hungary, saw a 19-year-old Johan Cruyff score on his international debut.

In the knock-out quarter-finals England met 1964 champions Spain with late goals by Bobby Charlton at Wembley and Norman Hunter in Madrid securing victory in both legs. An off-the-pace Italy were fortunate to pip Bulgaria thanks to a low-hit Angelo Domenghini free-kick. The Soviet Union turned around a 2-0 first leg defeat in Hungary and 21-year-old winger Dragan Džajić inspired a 6-2 aggregate rout for Yugoslavia over France.

With the semi-finalists decided, Italy were selected as host for the ensuing tournament. In the pouring rain in Naples, the first match pitted the home nation against the USSR. The great goalkeeper Dino Zoff made his second ever appearance for the Azzurri and his saves kept Italy in a tight and goalless game for 90 minutes. Despite being down to nine fit men, Italy finally came alive in extra-time, but it was the Soviet keeper Yuri Pshenichnikov's turn to save his team. It remained 0-0 and, with penalty shoot-outs yet to be introduced, the captains repaired to the referee's changing room to decide the match on the toss of a coin. In the stands, 68,000 Italian fans waited expectantly and eventually let out a mighty cheer as their captain Giancinto Facchetti emerged punching the air in delight.

The match in Naples was no footballing exhibition. This was perhaps slightly excusable given the atrocious weather and the fact that Italy, already missing gifted forward Luigi Riva, had playmaker Giani Riviera reduced to a bystander by injury. However, it was overshadowed by the defensive mentality and borderline thuggery on display in the other semi-final, between England and Yugoslavia in Florence. There were almost 50 free-kicks awarded and Alan Mullery, retaliating after a vicious kick, became the first ever Englishman to be sent off while playing for his country.

The game itself lacked sparkle. Once again, Džajić was Yugoslavia's main threat and it was he who broke the deadlock just four minutes from time. Nipping between Bobby Moore and goalkeeper Banks, he chested the ball down and flicked it home. The game summed up the whole tournament thus far: teams were defensive and unambitious to the point of dullness and games were over-physical and brutal. Two already exhausted and battered teams were due to meet in the final just three days later and expectations were low.

EUROPEAN CHAMPIONSHIP 1968 — 73

Despite wearng the number ten shirt, Giacinto Facchetti was one of the greatest full-backs of all time. He captained Italy 70 times, including both of the 1968 finals in Rome

THE HISTORY OF THE EUROPEAN CHAMPIONSHIP

1968 FINAL
Italy 1-1 Yugoslavia (a.e.t.)
Italy 2-0 Yugoslavia (replay)

England beat the USSR in the third place play-off with goals from World Cup heroes Charlton and Geoff Hurst, but the 69,000 spectators at the Stadio Olympico in Rome were only there for the main course: Italy versus Yugoslavia. Although both were cautious in their approach, they were clearly the best two teams in Europe and the final was more entertaining than many in the competition, if no thriller.

It was an even game with Džajić opening the scoring after 39 minutes, having uncharacteristically miscontrolled the ball before stabbing it past Zoff. Italy huffed and puffed, but were fortunate when Vahidin Musemić passed rather than shot into an open goal. It was barely deserved, but another rasping Domenghini free-kick with ten minutes remaining bought Italy a replay, the first ever in a European Championship final.

Less than half the original crowd returned to the stadium two days later for the re-match. Yugoslavia were now missing two of their best players in Ilija Petković and Ivica Osim, while Italy brought back the creative Giancarlo De Sisti, Sandro Mazzola who had been rested and, returning from injury, 'The Thunderclap', super-striker Gigi Riva. It was enough against exhausted opponents. Džajić failed to shine for once and Italy took control. Riva turned on a loose ball after a corner to strike early and on the half-hour Pietro Anastasi flicked the ball up and sent a superb volley into the net. Italy never lost control and their captain and player of the tournament, Facchetti, hoisted the trophy. Once again, the host nation had triumphed.

MAGIC MOMENTS
FLIP OF A COIN

'It's all over. Facchetti is a lucky man!' Italy's Burgnich reportedly said when he discovered his captain would call the coin toss that decided their semi-final result. When referee Tschenscher flipped the coin, Facchetti jumped in to call 'Tails!' and proved his teammate right.

Italian captain Giacinto Facchetti lifts the Henri Delaunay Cup after the 1968 European Championship final against Yugoslavia, June 1968

EUROPEAN CHAMPIONSHIP 1968

THE HISTORY OF THE EUROPEAN CHAMPIONSHIP

EUROPEAN CHAMPIONSHIP 1972

BELGIUM

West Germany went into their first ever European Championship finals as favourites, having emerged in the qualifiers as a free-passing force full of movement and adventure. They had top-quality players in captain Franz Beckenbauer and goalkeeper Sepp Maier, the world's best striker in Gerd Müller and exciting young players in full-back Paul Breitner and midfielder Uli Hoeness. Most of all they had Günter Netzer, another midfielder, whose brilliance ignited an already dominant team.

West Germany had humiliated England in a 3-1 victory at Wembley to make the final tournament. They were joined by Hungary, who had dispensed with Romania in the quarter-finals; USSR, who saw off a moribund version of 1968 finalists Yugoslavia; and Belgium, who managed to defeat champions Italy in the second leg in Brussels, despite losing star player Wilfried van Moer with a broken leg.

Belgium were selected as finals hosts as UEFA continued with a four-team tournament. The only modifications were the introduction of red and yellow cards and an allowance of two substitutes per team each match. The USSR faced Hungary in Brussels in front of just 1,659 spectators, the smallest ever attendance in the history of the finals. For much of the match those staying away looked to have made the right decision with a couple of scrappy chances for each side the only excitement.

After 53 minutes they finally had a contest. A Soviet corner was headed out to the edge of the area where it was met by Anatoliy Konkov, who struck a deflected half-volley through a crowded area to give USSR the lead. Hungary failed to mount much of a response, but somehow an unlikely reprieve arose when they were awarded a penalty with just five minutes remaining. However, Sándor Zámbó's kick was saved and László Szőke failed to convert the rebound. Without much excitement a functional USSR had reached their third European Championship final out of four.

Simultaneously, in Antwerp, the host nation had kicked off against the fancied West Germany, who seemed to have the support of a majority of the 55,000 crowd. After conceding an early chance that Belgium's Raoul Lambert put just wide, the Green Machine (Germany in their now famous away kit) clicked into gear. Netzer began to run the game. On 24 minutes his floated ball into the Belgium area was met by Müller, whose flicked header flew into the top corner. In response, Belgium managed to create a couple of half-chances that forced Maier to save, but struggled to retain control of the ball.

It was the same Netzer–Müller combination that enabled West Germany to double the lead on 72 minutes. The playmaker sent a magnificent pass from the halfway line into the penalty area where the lethal striker stabbed the ball past the Belgium keeper. The match was effectively over with only Odilon Polleunis' cracking shot into the roof of the net providing a late consolation for the home spectators.

EUROPEAN CHAMPIONSHIP 1972 — 77

Jupp Heynckes (r), Günter Netzer (10), Franz Beckenbauer (centre) and Gerd Müller (l) celebrate West Germany's second goal in the 1972 semi-fina against Belgium

THE HISTORY OF THE EUROPEAN CHAMPIONSHIP

1972 FINAL: West Germany 3-0 Soviet Union

Brussels' Heysel Stadium, overlooked by the landmark Atomium, was the venue for the final between West Germany and the USSR. Beckenbauer's team played with style and dynamism, while a pragmatic USSR were missing some of their best players through injury. Just a month before, West Germany had beaten them 4-1 in a friendly in Munich. Few expected anything different in Belgium and that was the way it went.

Netzer and Beckenbauer seemed free to roam the pitch and Müller was always hovering dangerously. The team passed the ball with an instinctive fluidity, attacking and exhilarating, and a precursor of the Netherlands' Total Football. The Soviet team couldn't live with them and the first half was an onslaught. Shots rained in. Müller and Breitner's efforts were well saved by Yevhen Rudakov, while Hoeness' diving header hit the woodwork. When Netzer's acrobatic volley from outside the box cannoned off the bar, it was headed out to Jupp Heynckes, whose half-volley was saved, but only fell to the deadly Müller. The USSR were thankful to reach half-time just one goal down.

They fared no better in the second half. On 52 minutes a string of a dozen passes ended with unsung midfielder Herbert Wimmer sliding a shot across Rudakov for the second. Just six minutes later it was all over. An exchange of passes in the USSR area landed at Müller's feet and he gratefully swept in his third in the finals, and 11th including the qualifiers. West Germany were the deserved champions with a welcome triumph for attacking football and arguably still the greatest performance seen in a Euro final.

MAGIC MOMENTS
SPIN TO WIN

The superb pivot and shot by Gerd Müller that gave West Germany an emphatic 3-1 quarter-final victory at Wembley over England was a statement. It was the first time any German side had beaten England on English soil and marked the arrival of a scintillating team.

EUROPEAN CHAMPIONSHIP 1972 — 79

West Germany's team captain Franz Beckenbauer poses with the trophy after their 1972 triumph in Brussels

EUROPEAN CHAMPIONSHIP 1976

Qualification for the 1976 finals was fiercely contested with Poland (the third placed team in the 1974 World Cup), England and Italy missing out in the group phase, and Wales, having topped their group for the first ever time, Belgium, Spain and the USSR, who had been the only team to have reached every final tournament, exiting in the quarter finals.

In advance, many seemed sure of the way the four-team tournament would unfold. The 1974 World Cup finalists – West Germany and the Netherlands – were drawn in separate semi-finals and were expected to meet again after that. However, both had internal issues. Disagreements had left West Germany without the super-striker Gerd Müller and the star of the 1972 championships, Gunter Netzer, while Netherlands were racked by in-fighting with coach George Knobel even attempting to resign on the morning of the semi-final. This meant that fans were lucky enough to witness two of the most exciting and entertaining games in the competition to date.

In a rain-lashed Zagreb, Netherlands underestimated their opponents Czechoslovakia, who had gone 17 games without defeat. The underdogs attacked from the start and Anton Ondruš' header from Antonin Panenka's chipped free-kick gave them a deserved early lead. As the game became increasingly scrappy, referee Clive Thomas struggled to maintain control. Jaroslav Pollák was eventually sent off on the hour for a nasty hack on Neeskens and just 15 minutes later the Dutchman followed him for a crude foul on Zdeněk Nehoda.

Between the two red cards, the Netherlands had equalised courtesy of an Ondruš miscued volley into his own net. The Oranje then pressed for a winner, but Czechoslovakia's keeper Ivo Viktor kept them at bay. Extra-time saw Czechoslovakia rouse themselves and they were rewarded in the 114th minute when a long cross was headed home by an unmarked Nehoda at the far post. When Netherlands' Wim van Hanegem was sent off for dissent, their dejection was clear and it was no surprise when a cute pass from Panenka left František Veselý to easily round the keeper and seal a 3-1 victory.

In Belgrade, another upset seemed on the cards. Yugoslavia, to all accounts a team in decline, immediately put the World Champions to the sword. Danila Popivoda outpaced Franz Beckenbauer enabling the Yugoslavs to take the lead and Dragan Džajić scrambled in a Sepp Maier fumble for a second on the half-hour. However, in the second half, fortune presented West Germany with a way back as Heinz Flohe's shot from distance cannoned off Herbert Wimmer to leave the keeper stranded.

Back in the game at 2-1, West Germany came to life. With 11 minutes remaining they sent on striker Dieter Müller for his debut. Within three minutes he had levelled the scores, heading home with his first touch. Extra-time came and both sides looked for a winner. Just five minutes remained when Müller, unmarked again, hammered the ball into the roof of the net. Yugoslavia were down and out, but not before Rainer Bonhof drilled a shot against the post with the rebound falling to Müller, who recorded a remarkable hat-trick. West Germany had a new hero.

EUROPEAN CHAMPIONSHIP 1976 — 81

West Germany striker Uli Hoeness outpaces Jose Martinez Pirri of Spain during the 1976 quarter-final in Madrid

1976 FINAL: Czechoslovakia 2-2 West Germany (a.e.t.)
(Czechoslovakia won 5-3 on penalties)

Another exciting match ensued in the third-place play-off when Netherlands defeated Yugoslavia 3-2 in extra-time and, after 15 goals in three matches, there were high hopes for a gripping final. It didn't disappoint. After just eight minutes Czechoslovakia's Ján Švehlík was presented with an open goal and made no mistake. Then, when Karol Dobiaš' low, bobbling shot from the edge of the area doubled the lead near the half hour mark, Germany were shell-shocked, but they responded instantly, with new star Müller pulling one back with an acrobatic scissor-kick from just metres out.

For the rest of the match the Germans drove forward, but goalkeeper Viktor was having the game of his life. The final whistle was seconds away when Bernd Hölzenbein just beat him to Bonhof's corner to take the game to extra-time at 2-2. As Viktor continued his heroics through the remainder of the open play, he had every reason to think he could prevent West Germany winning the penalty shoot-out.

In fact, neither he nor West Germany's Maier managed to save any of the first seven penalties. With Czechoslovakia 4-3 up, Hoeness stepped up only to blast the ball sky high over the crossbar – and the rest is football legend. Panenka, needing to score to ensure victory, runs to the ball with intent. After the slightest of stutters, he gently clips the ball down the middle of the goal. Maier, sprawling to his left, looks round in dismay. Czechoslovakia have become kings of Europe in the most audacious way ever.

MAGIC MOMENTS
PRACTICE MAKES PERFECT

Antonin Panenka later explained he had come up with the idea of momentarily delaying his kick then chipping the ball down the middle months before, while brainstorming ideas to beat the keeper. He had then repeatedly practised the move, which culminated in that perfect penalty in Belgrade.

Karol Dobias of Czechoslovakia helps West Germany's Dieter Muller to his feet during the 1976 final in Belgrade

THE HISTORY OF THE EUROPEAN CHAMPIONSHIP

EUROPEAN CHAMPIONSHIP 1980

ITALY

After the excitement of the 1976 finals, UEFA decided to change the format for the 1980 edition. They picked the host nation – Italy – in advance and increased the number of teams taking part to eight in two groups of four. The semi-finals were scrapped and the winners of each group would go straight through to the tournament final. It proved a great error, though, as the group system only encouraged a defensive mentality and there was no potential for teams to go on what might be an exciting journey. With Italian football still rocked by a betting scandal and English fans bringing hooliganism to the cities and terraces, attendances were low and the mood gloomy.

Of the four nations in what was called Group 1, West Germany brought a very young side that included just one of their losing finalists from the 1976 European Championship in Bernard Dietz". On the other hand, the winners in that final, an ageing Czechoslovakian team, still fielded Panenka, Nehoda and Ondruš. The Netherlands, too, were in transition; they had quality veterans, but none of their Total Football stars. Greece gave every impression of making up the numbers.

And so it played out. After single-goal victories over Czechoslovakia and Greece respectively, the stage was set for the great European rivals, West Germany and the Netherlands, to lock horns. Although Klaus Alloffs scored a hat-trick as West Germany took a 3-0 lead, plaudits went to the 20-year-old midfielder Bernd Schuster, who was at the heart of all three. The Netherlands struck back with a penalty and a fabulous long-distance strike from Willy van der Kerkhof in the last two minutes, but it was too little too late. All Germany now needed was a draw with Greece to make another final, which they secured with little fuss and no goals.

Group 2 featured the hosts Italy whose best players were goalkeeper Dino Zoff, defenders Claudio Gentile and Gaetano Scirea, and the playmaker Giancarlo Antognoni; England, led by forward Kevin Keegan, then rated among Europe's best; the hard-to-beat Belgium, whose decision to bring back 35-year-old maestro Wilfried van Moer had proved an inspirational decision; and Spain, who had pipped Yugoslavia to qualify.

The ties were insipid and dull, shackled by cautious tactics and rough tackling. England, one of the more adventurous teams in the tournament, seemed subdued by the behaviour of their fans, while Italy desperately underperformed. Their meeting in Turin was supposed to be the highlight of the group stage, but Marco Tardelli's strike was the only goal in a tight game. Belgium were the surprise package of the tournament. They earned a draw with England when Jan Ceulemans cancelled out Ray Wilkins' sublime lob and beat Spain 2-1 in Milan. Well-organised and disciplined, they also had attacking potency in Ceulemans, Franky Van der Elst and René Vandereycken.

Only nine goals were scored in the Group 2 games as Italy and Belgium finished joint top. Italy, who had scored just once in their three ties, bowed out. Belgium, who played the defensive, streetwise game better than the rest, reached their first ever final by way of their three goals scored.

EUROPEAN CHAMPIONSHIP 1980 — 85

Tony Woodcock of England in action against Italy during their 1980 group stage encounter in Turin

1980 FINAL: West Germany 2-1 Belgium

The final in the Stadio Olimpico in front of 47,864 spectators went a little way to offsetting a dour tournament. That was mainly due to the flair of West Germany who, in Schuster, Hansi Müller and Karl-Heinz Rummenigge, had the best creative players on show, but some credit is due to Belgium, too, who made a match of what was expected to be a one-sided game.

It looked that way after 10 minutes when striker Horst Hrubresch smashed the ball home after a perfect chipped pass from Schuster. The young midfielder was irrepressible for the rest of the half, delivering a host of chances. The second half had hardly got going, however, when Belgium's François van der Elst, possibly still outside the area, was brought down by West German defender Uli Stielke to win a penalty. René Vandereycken sent keeper Toni Schumacher the wrong way to convert and Belgium were back in the game.

Marshalled by Eric Gerets, one of the tournament's best defenders, Belgium remained forthright. Despite Schuster and Rummenigge both going close, they failed to beat keeper Jean-Marie Pfaff, who had saved his best game for the final. Extra-time was just 90 seconds away when Rummenigge's beautifully flighted corner caught Pfaff in two minds. In a split-second, Hrubresch arrived to nod home from close range: his second goal and the match winner. West Germany became the first team to win multiple titles and, with an average age of just 25 years and 136 days, they remain the youngest side to emerge victorious from a European Championship final.

MAGIC MOMENTS
BULLET HEADER

West Germany's Horst Hrubresch scored twice in the final against Belgium and the second – and decisive – goal was one of his trademark bullet headers. As a player he was known as the 'Header Beast' and that strike confirmed the nickname.

Manfred Kaltz of Germany celebrates their win over Belguim during the UEFA European Championships 1980 Final, June 22, 1980

EUROPEAN CHAMPIONSHIP 1984

FRANCE

As hosts of the 1984 European Football Championship the French qualified automatically. They and the other seven teams were then divided into two groups of four, and they met Denmark in the opening game. The most memorable incident of this match came just before half-time, when veteran Danish striker Allan Simonsen instantly ended his tournament by breaking his leg in a clash with French defender Yvon Le Roux. Despite that, it was all fairly evenly balanced until just over ten minutes from the end, when Michel Platini, widely held to be one of the greatest footballers ever and then at the height of his powers, put one past Danish keeper Ole Qvist.

Platini was just warming up, though, and scored hat-tricks against both the other teams in Group A, Belgium and Yugoslavia. France's maximum points ensured they went forward, as did the Danes, who beat the other two sides as well. Group B generated fewer goals and was largely notable for West Germany's failure to progress. Instead, they and Romania went out, and Spain and Portugal went through to the next round.

The France and Portugal semi-final is widely held to be one of the best matches of any European Championship ever. The French coach crashed on the way to Marseille's Stade Vélodrome. Fortunately, no one was seriously injured, but it wasn't an auspicious start and when the game got underway the first 20 minutes were dull, until Jaime Pacheco brought Platini down 25 metres from the Portuguese goal. A free-kick was given and keeper Manuel Bento was left standing as Jean-François Domergue blasted the ball into the top corner. The French were 1-0 up.

They sat on their lead until the break, but came out for the second half all guns blazing. Platini had a shot and Alain Giresse came close three times in five minutes, but the next goal arrived at the other end. Fernando Chalana delivered the ball neatly into the French box and Rui Jordão's header beat keeper Joël Bats, appearing at his first international tournament. After 74 minutes it was 1-1. After 90 minutes the scoreline hadn't changed, so it went to extra-time. The French looked like they were tiring and on 98 minutes Jordão swiftly fired in another from another nicely weighted Chalana cross.

This galvanised the French and they discovered new reserves of energy, but still they found it hard to break through Portugal's now tightly closed ranks. There were only six minutes of the game left when João Pinto brought down Platini in the box and while the referee was wondering whether the Frenchman had dived or not, Domergue picked up the ball and side-footed it over Bento to level the game at 2-2. Penalties loomed, but with just 90 seconds left on the clock, the tireless Jean Tigana made a last-gasp run, delivering the ball to a composed Platini, who was waiting in front of the Portuguese goal and who placed his shot into the top of the net. France had beaten Portugal 3-2 after extra-time and were through to the final.

The other semi-final, between Spain and Denmark in Lyon, was not quite as memorable, but it was still an exciting, incident-filled game. The Danes scored after just 7 minutes, when Søren Lerby picked up a loose ball and stuck it in from close quarters. They had a strong plea for a penalty turned down, but although they made chances, they couldn't seem to finish them off and paid for it in the second half when Antonio Maceda tipped another loose ball into the bottom corner of the net. Extra-time produced no further goals, so it went down to a close penalty shoot-out, which Spain won 5-4.

EUROPEAN CHAMPIONSHIP 1984

Spanish keeper Luis Arconada foils a Danish attack with a spectacular save during the 1984 semi-final in Lyon

THE HISTORY OF THE EUROPEAN CHAMPIONSHIP

1984 FINAL — France 2-0 Spain

It was almost inevitable that after two extraordinary semi-finals the final itself, played in a packed Paris at Parc des Princes, would be somewhat less than enthralling – and so it proved. France looked lacklustre, Spain looked exhausted, but the French had a spot of luck and just over ten minutes into the second half Spanish keeper Luis Arconada let a low shot from Platini slip over the line.

This energised the home side and they finally started to perform, but five minutes before full-time Le Roux was sent off for a second bookable offence. The Spanish couldn't capitalise on this, though, and an injury-time goal from Bruno Bellone made the final score 2-0 to the home team.

France had won their first major international trophy, but, more than that, 1984 had been a fantastically successful event, both on and off the pitch, and, after the lows of 1980, it had ensured that the European Championship as a tournament would survive.

MAGIC MOMENTS
GOAL MACHINE

Michel Platini's 57th-minute free-kick, which gave France the lead in the final against Spain, meant that he had scored in every match of the competition – two headers, two free-kicks, one penalty and four shots in open play. His nine goals in one tournament still stand as a record.

EUROPEAN CHAMPIONSHIP 1984

France's national coach Michel Hidalgo being carried on the shoulders of the French players with the trophy, 1984 final

EUROPEAN CHAMPIONSHIP 1988

WEST GERMANY

They had won in 1984 and it was something of a shock when France failed to qualify for the 1988 tournament. Other notable absentees were Portugal and Belgium. Instead, hosts West Germany were joined by Italy, Denmark and Spain in Group A; and England, first-time qualifiers the Republic of Ireland, the Soviet Union and the Netherlands in Group B.

In the opening game the Italians held the West Germans to a tight 1-1 draw, but West Germany managed to top the group on goal difference with Italy, who had scored just one goal less, going through in second place. In the other group, the Republic of Ireland started out with a surprise win over England, but the USSR and Netherlands proved the stronger teams, the Soviets finishing with a point more than the Dutch.

West Germany met the Netherlands in the first semi-final and again the game was tight until, ten minutes into the second half, Jürgen Klinsmann was fouled in the box by Frank Rijkaard and the West Germans appealed for a penalty. Some said Klinsmann dived, but it was given and Lothar Matthäus converted it. Maybe the referee regretted that decision, because 20 minutes later, when Jürgen Kohler brought down Marco van Basten, he gave one the other way, even though Van Basten got straight back up and looked rather nonplussed. Naturally he didn't protest, though, and Ronald Koeman scored from the spot to make it 1-1. Extra-time looked like inevitability until, on 89 minutes, Van Basten suddenly picked up a pass from Jan Wouters, outpaced Kohler and poked the ball home past keeper Eike Immel. Somewhat against expectations, the Netherlands were in the final.

The other semi-final – USSR versus Italy – also delivered quite an upset. The Italians were favourites, but despite taking charge of the game and generating lots of goal-scoring opportunities, they failed to capitalise on those chances. They probably lacked the experience of their opponents, too, who tackled and worked hard. That toughness was rewarded when, a quarter of an hour or so into the second half, Hennadiy Lytovchenko and Oleg Protasov both beat Walter Zenga on the counter-attack. It stayed at 2-0 and the Soviets would join the Dutch in the final.

EUROPEAN CHAMPIONSHIP 1988 — 93

Jürgen Kohler of Germany and Marco van Basten of the Netherlands battle for the ball during the 1988 semi-final in Hamburg

1988 FINAL: Netherlands 2-0 Soviet Union

The USSR could have taken an early lead at Munich's Olympiastadion. Lytovchenko went wide after just two minutes and after 30 minutes he shot straight at Dutch keeper Hans van Breukelen. Three minutes later, though, Erwin Koeman took a Dutch corner. It was headed away, but Koeman scooped up the loose ball and sent it into the box. Van Basten nodded it on as the Soviets pushed out to play offside, leaving captain Ruud Gullit to run in and head the ball past goalie Rinat Dasaev. The Netherlands were leading 1-0.

The USSR should have equalised before half-time, but Igor Belanov skimmed it over the crossbar and ten minutes after the restart the Dutch went 2-0 up. It was an absolutely sensational goal – undoubtedly one of the best ever scored in a European Championship game. Arnold Mühren's over-hit cross reached van Basten well beyond the far post only for the tournament's top-scorer to volley with his right foot from a ridiculously implausible angle, to send the ball straight into the net.

It was 2-0, but the Dutch weren't home and dry yet. Belanov hit the post and came close, and then just before the hour mark Erwin Koeman failed to clear the ball properly and Protasov headed it back wide of his opponents' goal. Sergei Gotsmanov managed to keep it in play, but was foolishly fouled by Van Breukelen. Belanov stepped up to take the penalty. Having given it away, the pressure on the Dutch goalie to save it was immense, but amazingly he dived in the right direction and did. After that the Soviets seemed to lose heart and when the whistle blew the Dutch were European champions for the first time.

The 1988 tournament had been professional and successful, and was also notable because it had no goalless draws, no extra-time, no converted penalties and no red cards either. In effect, this meant that the eight qualifying teams had all been of a broadly similar standard, apart from perhaps the Danes, who were acknowledged to be a side in decline.

Also, no matches in this tournament were played in West Berlin, because the Soviet Union and other Eastern Bloc countries disputed that it was part of West Germany. However, this final was the Soviet Union's last European Championship game under that name and it ceased to exist after 1991, and indeed 1990's reunification had made West Germany and East Germany one nation again.

EUROPEAN CHAMPIONSHIP 1988 — 95

Arnold Muhren raises the trophy after the Netherlands victory over the Soviet Union in the 1988 final in Munich

MAGIC MOMENTS

GOING ROUTE ONE

Marco van Basten looked at the three defenders between him and the goal and thought, 'I can stop the ball and do things with all these players or I could do it the easier way.' The result was one of the most iconic goals of all time.

EUROPEAN CHAMPIONSHIP 1992

The last European Championship with the eight-team format, this tournament was held in Sweden. To mark the occasion, the Swedish FA commissioned Abba's Benny Andersson to compose a signature tune for the competition. It's not 'Mama Mia', but it's a jaunty little number nonetheless, which you can find on YouTube.

The hosts qualified as a matter of course. The Soviet Union had originally qualified, but even though it no longer existed as a nation, it appeared as the CIS or Commonwealth of Independent States with players drawn from almost all parts of the former USSR. The Yugoslavs had also qualified, but war in the Balkans meant that it no longer existed as a country either. It was a fraught situation and ten days before Euro 1992 was set to kick off, Yugoslavia was disqualified. Already in Sweden, the squad had to fly home and the spare place was given to Denmark.

The early games in Group A were characterised by a series of draws. Sweden managed 1-1 against a disjointed French side; it was 0-0 when England played Denmark; and the same when England played France. This was an England side managed by Graham Taylor and captained by Gary Lineker, but key players like Paul Gascoigne and Tony Adams were missing due to injury, and the team failed to live up to expectations. In the final two group fixtures, Sweden beat England 2-1, the English goal coming early on from David Platt, and the Danes scored a surprise 2-1 against the French. England and France were going home. Sweden and Denmark were going forward.

In Group B, Scotland managed to beat a CIS team who were, unsurprisingly given recent political events, unsettled. That game finished 3-0 to the Scots, whereas Germany and the Netherlands only achieved draws with the CIS team, 0-0 and 1-1 respectively. The Germans beat Scotland 2-0, but the Netherlands beat Germany 3-1, the latter undoubtedly the game of the group stage. Jürgen Klinsmann scored for the Germans. The Dutch goals came from Frank Rijkaard, Rob Witschge and a new kid on the block called Dennis Bergkamp. Those two sides topped the group. Scotland and the CIS were out.

Germany had been coasting. They had to find their form in the semi-final against Sweden and they did. An energised captain Andreas Brehme, the full-back who had scored the winning penalty against Argentina to raise the 1990 World Cup, led the charge and Germany's Thomas Häßler scored first. Then Karl-Heinz Riedle made it 2-0 to Germany, but 20 minutes into the second half Klas Ingesson was brought down by Thomas Helmer and the Swedes were awarded a penalty, which was smoothly converted by Tomas Brolin. However, in the 89th minute Helmer set up Riedle for a third German goal and despite a literally last-minute header from Kennet Andersson, the Germans were through, 3-2.

In the second semi-final, perhaps the Dutch felt the pressure and the Danes felt they had nothing to lose. Certainly, Denmark refused to be intimidated and

Jurgen Klinsmann (L) in action for Germany during their 3-2 victory over Sweden in the Euro 1992 semi-final

were the first to score, with a header from Henrik Larsen. The Netherlands equalised when Bergkamp got the better of Peter Schmeichel in the Danish goal, but Larsen got another by smashing in a loose ball after Ronald Koeman stopped a Brian Laudrup header – and all this before half-time. The Dutch became increasingly desperate, but it stayed at 2-1 to Denmark until the 86th minute, when Rijkaard finally hit the back of the net. At 2-2 extra-time followed and then penalties, which, after the Netherlands' Marco van Basten missed, were won 5-4 by the Danes.

THE HISTORY OF THE EUROPEAN CHAMPIONSHIP

1992 FINAL — Denmark 2-0 Germany

In the final, Germany, the tournament favourites, faced Denmark, the team who were more or less there to make up the numbers. The Germans got off to a good start and created several decent chances, but it was the Danes who, at 20 minutes in, scored first. John Jensen was a hardworking central midfielder. He was known for being erratic in front of goal, but on this occasion he struck it beautifully and with deadly accuracy. As the teams went in at half-time Demark led Germany 1-0. However, after the break, the Germans could have led the Danes by two, if not three, but they just couldn't get past Schmeichel. Denmark had chances, too, and 12 minutes from the end, on the break, Kim Vilfort's shot hit the post and went in. It was a famous upset, an absolute sensation, a fairy-tale ending – they hadn't even qualified originally, yet Denmark were the champions of Europe!

MAGIC MOMENTS
COMETH THE MAN

John Jensen was Denmark's hard-working midfielder. Known for his erratic shooting he had made 42 appearances for his country and was still to score. He had saved it for the perfect moment: a thunderous 20-metre strike that stunned Germany and inspired his team to go on and win the final.

EUROPEAN CHAMPIONSHIP 1992 — 99

Denmark celebrate a second goal against Germany that sealed their 1992 European Championship triumph

THE HISTORY OF THE EUROPEAN CHAMPIONSHIP

EURO 96

ENGLAND

'Football's coming home' was the theme set by England as they hosted the tenth European Championship, now officially with the new catchy name of Euro 96. UEFA had introduced three points for a win, a golden goal decider in extra-time and extended the format to include 16 nations, including a reunified Germany, and the Czech Republic and Croatia playing for the first time in a tournament as independent nations.

The group stages were tightly fought with no team winning all three matches. Early to impress were Germany who, with sweeper Matthias Sammer and striker Jürgen Klinsmann looking sharp, opened with victories over the Czech Republic and Russia. In the 'group of death', the Czechs' 2-1 victory over Italy saw them take second spot. Meanwhile, Portugal's blossoming 'golden generation', led by Luis Figo with Fernando Couto, Paulo Sousa and Rui Costa, made a good case for being the dangerous outsiders. They finished ahead of Croatia, for whom Davor Šuker scored the most delicate chip ever over Peter Schmeichel in their crucial 3-0 win over Denmark.

France and Spain qualified from Group B without fanfare and Bulgaria, for whom the temperamental but brilliant Hristo Stoichkov scored in each of their games, bowed out. Romania, even with Gheorghe Hagi's flashes of his genius, failed to win a point. England began slowly with an opening draw with Switzerland and a poor first half against Scotland at Wembley. Even a 53rd minute Alan Shearer-headed goal from a Gary Neville cross failed to raise them. When Scotland were awarded a penalty, the hosts looked to be crumbling.

Everything changed in two minutes. David Seaman saved from Gary McAllister's spot kick and 90 seconds later Paul Gascoigne, who many had dismissed as finished, flicked the ball over Stephen Hendry's head with his left foot and volleyed home with his right. It – along with his hilarious dentist's chair celebration – changed the mood immediately. England now topped the group and thrashed a much-fancied Netherlands team (again racked with internal feuds) 4-1, with Shearer notching another two goals.

The group stage had produced plenty of goals and England's newfound optimism created a buzz around the tournament. However, the knockout stages were a different story with the golden goal rule – intended to make extra-time exciting – backfiring. The first quarter-final, featuring England and Spain, was intriguing. The host nation were purring while Spain, despite underperforming in the group stage, had gone 19 games without being beaten. A raucous Wembley, however, saw a goalless damp squib. Spain were the better team with only Seaman and a generous offside decision keeping England in it. Extra-time and the promise of a golden goal came and went. Both sides were more concerned with not conceding than scoring. The only surprise was England winning a penalty shoot-out with more heroics from Seaman.

France against the Netherlands followed a similar pattern. It was a game of few chances and no goals, and the 30 minutes of extra-time were wasted, but Clarence Seedorf's tame penalty enabled the French to proceed in the tournament. Germany finally netted a quarter-final goal in their tie against Croatia with a Klinsmann penalty and Šuker, a constant danger, equalised with another deft piece of skill as he rounded the keeper just after half-time. However, within eight minutes the match was all but over, as Igor Štimac received a red card and Sammer's cool

Paul Gascoigne shoots to score England's second goal against Scotland at Wembley Stadium on June 15, 1996

Karel Poborsky scores the first goal of the match against Portugal on June 23, 1996

finish put Germany 2-1 up. The Germans were through, but in a rough game their inspirational captain Klinsmann had hobbled off and would miss the semi-final.

Portugal against Czech Republic was marked by a single moment of pure class. Speedy winger Karel Poborský picked up the ball in the Portuguese half and ran at the defenders, with some skill and some fortune he made it to the edge of the area, where he scooped the ball high over the oncoming keeper and watched it sail into the net.

France met the Czech Republic at Old Trafford in a semi-final that promised much and delivered little. With the Czech team depleted by injuries, France were expected to force the issue, but aside from Djorkaeff hitting the bar with a dipping shot, they created few chances. Extra-time again felt the weight of golden goals, so when substitute Reynald Pedros had the first of France's sudden penalties saved, it was left to skipper Miroslav Kadlec to smash his down the centre and put the Czechs in the final.

And so to Wembley, where England, drawn as the away side, looked out of place in an unappealing grey-blue kit. The 'Football's coming home' song rang out in the stands and after three minutes it looked possible when Shearer struck again with his head, this time from a Gascoigne corner. Germany regrouped. Stand-in captain Andreas Möller marshalled his team and after 19 minutes, Klinsmann's deputy Stephan Kuntz side-footed home from a metre out. The match ebbed and flowed. Both teams looked dangerous. Shearer put two headers just wide, Thomas Helmer sent a shot over the bar from 12 metres, Gascoigne began to show his class and Dieter Eilts was everywhere. There was no golden goal fear here in extra-time as Darren Anderton hit the post, Kuntz had a headed goal disallowed, Shearer's 99th minute ball across the face of goal passed the German keeper and Gascoigne's desperate lunge failed to connect and send the ball into an open net. Both teams tried to win the game with chances at both ends, but a shoot-out seemed inevitable. An impeccable five penalties left sudden death. When Gareth Southgate's soft shot was saved, it was left to Möller to seal the win in an epic match.

Stuart Pearce consoles Gareth Southgate after his penalty is saved during the Euro 96 semi final against Germany at Wembley Stadium on June 26, 1996

THE HISTORY OF THE EUROPEAN CHAMPIONSHIP

1996 FINAL — Germany 2-1 Czech Republic (a.e.t.)
(Germany won on a Golden Goal)

It was a final between two patched up and exhausted sides who did their best to put on a show. For Germany, Klinsmann returned despite not being fully fit and Kuntz kept his place after a fine performance against England. For the Czech Republic, star Karel Poborský was joined by a now fit Patrik Berger and a young Pavel Nedvěd, who had announced himself at the tournament.

In the first half, Germany were held at bay by Czech keeper Petr Kouba, who saved twice from Kuntz, but their opponents kept themselves in the game. Their reward came on the hour when a flying Poborský was upended by Sammer on the edge of the box and a penalty was awarded. Berger hammered home the kick and put the Czechs 1-0 up. Getting desperate, German coach Berti Vogts responded by bringing on striker Oliver Bierhoff for just his eighth appearance. A little more than ten minutes remained when the substitute appeared unmarked to head in an equaliser from Christian Ziege's free-kick.

For the first time in a Euro final, they went to golden goals. Initially it looked like a familiar scenario was being played out. Then, after five minutes, a long punt was flicked on by Bierhoff to Klinsmann whose cross returned the ball to him. Bierhoff, just inside the area, had his back to goal, but managed to turn and get a shot in. Kouba, perhaps unsighted, got both hands to it, but could only palm it into the inside netting. The tournament finally had its golden goal and its 1996 champions in the shape of Germany.

Swept along by fervent home support, the tournament had been a success, despite the failed golden goal experiment. Zinédine Zidane, Hristo Stoichkov, Gheorghe Hagi and Paul Gascoigne had shown their class; the new nations in Croatia and Czech Republic had earned respect; and Germany, just like West Germany before them, had shown they had the mentality and quality to triumph.

MAGIC MOMENTS
DENTIST'S CHAIR

Paul Gascoigne's goal against Scotland was memorable enough, but his celebration is arguably as famous. The 'dentist's chair' depicted a controversial night on England's pre-Euro tour in Hong Kong, where 'Gazza' and other players were reported to have been tied to a chair and plied with alcohol.

Jürgen Klinsmann embraces Golden Goal scorer Oliver Bierhoff in the Euro 96 final, 30 June, 1996

THE HISTORY OF THE EUROPEAN CHAMPIONSHIP

EURO 2000

BELGIUM | NETHERLANDS

Often cited as one of the best international tournaments ever, the 2000 European Championship produced quality football and featured exciting games. For the first time, it took place in not one but two countries – Belgium and neighbouring Netherlands – but the 16-team format was retained, as was the golden goal rule. Forty-nine teams entered the competition originally, the hosts went through automatically and among the qualifiers were many familiar names, with only Norway and Slovenia appearing as debutants.

In Group A, outgoing champions Germany faced Romania, but it was an ageing Germany, lacking in the discipline usually displayed by German teams, and the game finished 1-1. Indeed, Mehmet Scholl's curving shot turned out to be the only goal of Germany's tournament. They lost both of their other games, came bottom in the group and failed to make it to the next round. This was undoubtedly a low point for German football and the start of a plan to rebuild the German national side.

England, now coached by former player Kevin Keegan, managed to beat the Germans 1-0, due to a Shearer header. However, that was their only win, they didn't progress either and – somewhat surprisingly – it was Portugal and Romania who went on to the quarter-finals.

In Group B it was Italy and Turkey who progressed, and Sweden and – again, slightly against expectations – hosts Belgium who were out. Spain and Yugoslavia topped Group C, with the game in which these two sides met being particularly dramatic and memorable (the final score was 4-3 to Spaniards). There was less excitement and upset in Group D, where it was the Netherlands and France who qualified for the quarters.

So now eight teams would be reduced to four. The first quarter-final was a fairly unremarkable affair in which Portugal dispensed with Turkey 2-0, both Portugal goals being scored by Nuno Gomes and set up by the extraordinary Luís Figo. Italy then took on Romania, a side the included the great attacking midfielder Gheorghe Hagi, now somewhat past the height of his career, who was fouled outrageously by Demetrio Albertini five minutes before the break. Had the Italian been sent off the result might have been different. But then again it might not and Hagi himself was sent off on the hour mark for two bookable offences. It finished 2-0 to the Italians, with goals from Francesco Totti and Filippo Inzaghi sealing it.

The Netherlands' intelligent passing game was much too much for the Yugoslavians and they beat them comprehensively in the third quarter-final. In fact, an entertaining rout would be an acceptable description, as the final scoreline was 6-1 to Holland. Patrick Kluivert got three, Marc Overmars got two and the other one was an own goal from Dejan Govedarica, although Savo Milošević did get one back in the 92nd minute.

The last quarter, between France and Spain, was fiercely fought and enjoyable to watch. Patrick Vieira and Christophe Dugarry missed opportunities to score from headers for France early on, which woke Spain up. Pep Guardiola took a curling free kick, which would have slipped in at the near post had Fabien

Nuno Gomes and Luís Figo celebrate a goal during the UEFA Euro 2000 Quarter Final match against Turkey at Johan Cruijff Arena on June 24, 2000

THE HISTORY OF THE EUROPEAN CHAMPIONSHIP

Portugal protest to referee Gunter Benko during the semi-final against France at the King Baudouin Stadium in Brussels, Belgium. 28 Jun 2000

Barthez not punched it away, but it was a free-kick at the other end, given away by Agustín Aranzábal and taken by Zinédine Zidane, that brought the first goal, just after the half-hour mark.

Just over five minutes later Spain were awarded a penalty, after Lilian Thuram had brought down Pedro Munitis, and Gaizka Mendieta converted it to equalise. Then, just before the half-time whistle went, Vieira's perfect pass was picked up by Youri Djorkaeff who controlled the ball, shot and scored. As they went in, France were back in the lead and, despite sterling efforts from the Spanish, that's how it stayed.

France were a different team in their semi-final against Portugal. They lacked the fluidity they had shown against the Spaniards and Gomes got the first goal, for Portugal, after 19 minutes, when, more or less out of nowhere he fired a half-volley at a surprised Barthez. This failed to galvanise France, though, and they didn't equalise until five minutes after the restart – Nicolas Anelka set up Thierry Henry who shot into the corner. At 1-1 neither team could break the deadlock and it went to extra-time, but no one seemed to have the energy and focus it would take to win this game.

Well, not until six minutes away from a penalty shootout, when Sylvain Wiltord trapped a loose ball that was headed for the byline and shot from an exceedingly tight angle. His shot found the hand of defender Abel Xavier, who was standing on the near post, and the referee, Günter Benkö from Austria, pointed to the spot. The Portuguese went ballistic, surrounding the ref and screaming at him. Their coach, Humberto Coelho, even got involved, trying to calm his players down.

While this was going on, almost unnoticed, Portugal's star player Figo walked off the pitch and down the tunnel, removing his shirt as he went, because he knew that if France converted the penalty it would be a golden goal and the game would end. Sure enough, when Zidane stepped up and scored that was it. France had won 2-1 and were headed to the final.

In the other semi-final, the Netherlands easily outclassed Italy, with all the Dutch attacks coming through a majestic Dennis Bergkamp. They had several plausible chances, but were unable to capitalise on them, even when Italy's Gianluca Zambrotta was sent off after 34 minutes. In the first half Alessandro Nesta held back Kluivert in the box, but Frank de Boer's penalty was saved by Italian keeper Francesco Toldo. In the second half Edgar Davids was brought down by Mark Iuliano, but Kluivert's soft spot kick hit the post. It was still 0-0 at full-time and still 0-0 after extra-time, so it went to a shootout, which the Italians won, 3-1.

Zinedine Zidane celebrates a goal as France defeat Portugal 2-1 in the semi final in Brussels, Belgium on June 28, 2000

THE HISTORY OF THE EUROPEAN CHAMPIONSHIP

2000 FINAL — France 2-1 Italy (a.e.t.)
(France won on a Golden Goal)

There had been some fantastic games in the 2000 competition and at first it looked as though the final, played at Rotterdam's De Kuip stadium, would be disappointing, with a nervy first half for both sides. Just after the break, Dino Zoff, the legendary Italian goalkeeper who was managing his national side, took off midfielder Stefano Fiore and put on striker Alessandro del Piero instead (at the time, the world's highest paid footballer). This must have been the right decision, because within two minutes Marco Delvecchio had scored and Italy were 1-0 up.

However, Italy couldn't get another, despite some good chances, and France couldn't get an equaliser either. There were seconds left on the clock when Barthez booted a free-kick right up the pitch. David Trezeguet, who had come on for Djorkaeff, nodded it on to Wiltord, who nutmegged Nesta. It should have been an easy save for Toldo, but he was slow and the ball bobbled into the back of the net. The score was level at 1-1.

As it went to extra-time, France now had the momentum and Italy looked exhausted. Just short of the midway point Fabio Cannavaro passed to Albertini, but the ball was intercepted by Robert Pirès, who had come on for Bixente Lizarazu just before full-time. He went on a marvellous meandering run, before passing to Trezeguet, who blasted into the roof of the Italian net. The golden goal rule still applied, so it was 2-1 to the French and game over. It had been an extremely successful tournament and, like West Germany in 1972 and 1974, France now held both European and World titles simultaneously.

MAGIC MOMENTS
 MAN IN BLACK

No one remembers the referee – unless it's Pierluigi Collina, the ref with the baldpate and bulging eyes who was a star of Euro 2000. The moment the ice-cool Italian went forehead to forehead with Czech hardman Tomáš Řepka, before staring him out and booking him, was just one of many to savour.

France with the trophy after the Euro 2000 Final against Italy at Feyenoord Stadium, Rotterdam, Netherlands on 02 July 2000

THE HISTORY OF THE EUROPEAN CHAMPIONSHIP

EURO 2004

PORTUGAL

It was a tournament that promised to match the quality shown four years earlier. With some of the world's best talent in David Beckham, Zinédine Zidane, Luís Figo and Raúl all on show, hopes were high. The footballing extravaganza never quite materialised, but Euro 2004 compensated with drama, great goals and plenty of surprises and upsets.

The opening game delivered a shock as Portugal were defeated 2-1 by a stubborn, counter-attacking Greece, with only an injury-time goal by Manchester United's 19-year-old Cristiano Ronaldo as consolation. Portugal revived to top the group, while another solid backs-to-the-wall performance from Greece against Spain was enough to send Raúl and his teammates home.

Champions France met England in the first Group B tie. A Lampard header put England ahead, but it was the power and pace of 18-year-old striker Wayne Rooney that stood out. Eventually, on 73 minutes, he won a penalty and, even though Fabien Barthez brilliantly saved David Beckham's spot-kick, England looked in control. Then, on 90 minutes, Zidane equalised with a superb curling free-kick and, three minutes later, he made no mistake when France were awarded a penalty. It was a result that helped France top the group with England, inspired by Rooney, who scored four in victories over Croatia and Switzerland, second as expected.

Group C proved to be the tightest of them all. Italy with Alessandro Del Piero and Andrea Pirlo were favourites, but an opening draw with Denmark stunted their progress. Next, they faced Sweden, who recalled Henrik Larsson from retirement to lead the line alongside Ajax's young striker Zlatan Ibrahimović. Italy dominated, but were only one goal to the good and a Swedish corner in the 85th minute saw Ibrahimović equalise with a delicious looping flick. Italy could still progress as long as Denmark and Sweden didn't draw by more than 1-1 in the final game. It was 2-2, the Italians cried conspiracy, but this was no fix: the teams traded 31 shots and 31 fouls.

Group D was the 'group of death', bringing together Germany, the Netherlands, the Czech Republic and underdogs Latvia. Fired by Ballon d'Or winner Pavel Nedvěd, Karel Poborský and Tomas Rosický, the Czechs romped home, winning all three matches. With Germany stumbling to a draw with Lativa, the Netherlands – who boasted quality in Edwin van de Saar, Jaap Stam, Edgar Davids, Clarence Seedorf, Arjen Robben and Ruud van Nistelrooy – met the Czechs in the key match. It was enthralling with both teams throwing men forward. The Oranje went 2-0 up in 20 minutes, but the Czechs were level on 71 minutes through a rocket from Milan Baros. With two minutes to go, Vladimír Šmicer tapped in the winner after van der Saar had only half-saved a low shot.

The Czech Republic continued to look impressive as they dispensed with Denmark 3-0 in the quarter-final. Inspired by Robben, the Netherlands were deserved winners of their knock-out tie against Sweden, but had to do it the hard way. After a far from dull 0-0 draw, where both sides hit the woodwork and Swedish keeper Andreas Isaksson had a blinder, Robben slotted in the winner in the shoot-out.

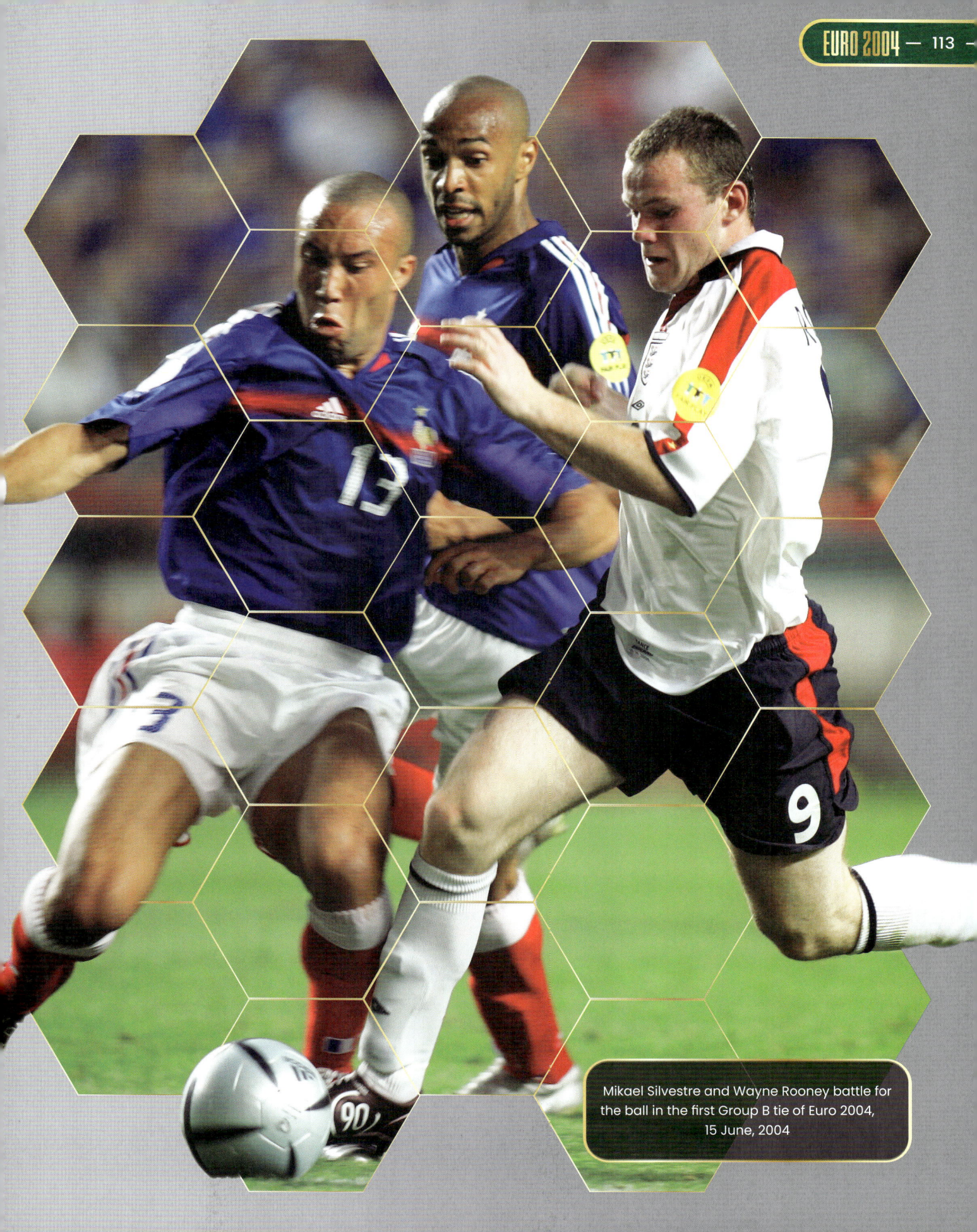

Mikael Silvestre and Wayne Rooney battle for the ball in the first Group B tie of Euro 2004, 15 June, 2004

THE HISTORY OF THE EUROPEAN CHAMPIONSHIP

In another thriller, Portugal against England also went to the wire. Michael Owen struck with a superb flicked shot after just three minutes, but when England's talisman Rooney limped off before the half hour mark, the tide turned. The Portuguese had a tight grip on the game with plenty of chances, but the equaliser remained elusive until Hélder Postiga headed home on 83 minutes. When Rui Costa's ripping shot from the edge of the area went in off the crossbar, England looked down and out, but they managed to take the match to penalties after Lampard's scrambled goal. At 4-4 in the shoot-out Darius Vassell's sudden-death shot was saved and Portugal goalkeeper Ricardo stepped-up to send the home fans wild as he hit the winner himself.

Amazingly, Greece's mixture of energy, organisation, good fortune and an ability to take their chances came good again against an underperforming France. The French, especially Thierry Henry, had plenty of scoring opportunities, but the Greeks were their equals. As France laboured, Greece's star men combined: Theodoros Zagorakis crossed for Angelos Charisteas to power a header home. The amazing Greek odyssey was not finished.

France's Thierry Henry (C) controls the ball ahead of Greece's Angelis Basinas, during the Euro 2004 quarter-finals at the Estadio Jose De Alvalade in Lisbon June, 25 2004

Cristiano Ronaldo of Portugal battles with Clarence Seedorf of Holland during the Euro 2004 Semi-Final at the Jose Alvalade Stadium, June 30, 2004

The first semi-final paired Portugal with the Netherlands and Figo's tournament finally came to life. He hit the post and set up two Ronaldo chances before teeing up the young star perfectly to head in from a corner. The Netherlands were still creating chances, but were hit with a thunderbolt when Maniche unleashed a curling strike from the corner of the penalty box that flew in just under the far post. Gifted a lifeline through a Jorge Andrade own goal, the Dutch pressed but, after a nail-biting climax, it finished 2-1 to Portugal and the hosts were in the final.

Upstarts Greece met the impressive Czech Republic in the other semi-final. Greece stuck to their tactics, defending stubbornly and pushing the rules with their tackling. When breached, they had keeper Antonios Nikopolidis to save them. Gradually they launched their own attacks. Despite losing star man Nedvěd to injury before the break, the Czechs were still on top, though looked vulnerable, but, goalless, a sometimes pulsating game went to extra time. Just seconds before the first period ended, Greece won a corner. Traianos Dellas lost his marker at the near post and glanced in a header. It was the first 'silver goal', an innovation introduced at this tournament in which the game ended if a team led at half-time in extra-time. With no time left for the Czechs to respond, it was certainly a golden moment for Greece.

THE HISTORY OF THE EUROPEAN CHAMPIONSHIP

2004 FINAL — Greece 1-0 Portugal

Portugal seemed certain winners. They had five Porto players who had just won the Champions League; flair players in Deco, Ronaldo, Figo and Rui Costa; an experienced coach in Phil Scolari who had won the World Cup with Brazil two years earlier; and a passionate home crowd roaring them on. Facing them were outsiders Greece. Otto Rehhagel's team was accused of being negative, over-physical and dull, their goals resulting from free-kicks, long throws and corners. They didn't care. They had already beaten Portugal in the tournament opener and knew they could do it again.

The hosts were on the front foot throughout the first half, but the Greek backline were as dogged and resilient as ever. In front of them the outstanding midfielder Zagorakis, later named player of the tournament, constantly broke up play and launched attacks. All Portugal managed to register were shots taken from a distance by Maniche, Pauleta and Miguel.

Greece's goal seemed inevitable as soon as they won a corner around the hour mark. It was a carbon copy of the goals that had sunk France and then the Czech Republic in the knock-out games. Angelis Basinas delivered a perfect out-swinging corner and Christeas rose between two defenders to meet it. Simple. Portugal tried to rouse themselves. Ronaldo created some half-chances for himself, but there was little to alarm Nikopolidis in the Greek goal. In the greatest upset that the European Championship had ever witnessed, Greece were champions.

Greece have been called the only underdogs in the history of football who everyone wanted to see beaten. However, defence is part of the game. Centre-back Dellas and right-back Giourkas Seitaridis both made the team of the tournament, but the whole back four deserved the acclaim. The stars might not have come out for Euro 2004, but the tournament had enough sparkle to live in the memory.

MAGIC MOMENTS
SILVER GOAL

The silver goal rule was very short-lived. Intended to reduce the likelihood of a penalty shoot-out but without the perceived unfairness of a golden goal, it was abolished after this tournament and Greece's semi-final winner was the only occasion it was used in a major international match.

Portuguese captain Luis Figo (C) tries to get through the Greek defence, during Euro 2004 Final, Estádio da Luz in Lisbon 04 July 2004

THE HISTORY OF THE EUROPEAN CHAMPIONSHIP

EURO 2008

AUSTRIA | SWITZERLAND

Austria and Switzerland were co-hosts in 2008 and there were no significant changes to the format. However, what was significant from a home nations point of view is that for the first time since 1984 there were no British or Irish representatives. That said, there were many familiar flags at the opening ceremony, with only host Austria and Poland new to the tournament.

England, managed by Steve McLaren, needed just a single point from their game against the already-through Croatia to qualify. However, they performed very poorly and lost 3-2. Scotland, drawn in a group that also contained France and Italy, faced an uphill struggle for qualification, but impressed by beating France in both legs and needed only a point against Italy. It was 1-1 as the clock wound down, but in the last seconds the referee gave a free kick the wrong way and Italy scored, robbing the Scots of their trip to the Alps. Northern Ireland had slayed some giants by beating Spain, Sweden and Denmark, but unaccountably lost to Iceland and Latvia, while Wales' best game was a 5-2 victory over Slovakia. The Republic of Ireland's campaign was similarly dismal.

In the first round of the tournament proper, Turkey and Portugal were the easy qualifiers from Group A, although Czech Republic notched a win over home side Switzerland in the opening game and in turn Switzerland beat Portugal, 2-1. In Group B, the Austrians came enthusiastically close to beating the Croatians, but were essentially out of their depth. In fact, Croatia won all their matches and topped the group, with Germany, who had the 2006 World Cup win under their belts and were clearly back in form again, second. Austria were able to salvage a little pride, though, as it was Poland who came bottom, on goal difference.

The Dutch were the clear winners of Group C, scoring nine goals and a maximum nine points. Italy were the runners-up, but their win against the French, draw with Italy and 3-0 loss to the Netherlands didn't cover them in glory, although they still had star players like Andrea Pirlo. Likewise, France had no Thierry Henry, but they did have Nicolas Anelka, Franck Ribéry and Karim Benzema. However, they performed very poorly, and they and the Romanians were very much also-rans. Finally, in Group D Spain sailed through all their matches and Russia, managed by the veteran Guus Hiddink, progressed, despite some erratic play and losing 4-1 to the Spanish. Sweden and Greece, who scored a solitary goal and failed to gain any points, were out.

The group stage had weeded out the weaker teams and it was a worthy set of sides who lined up for the quarter-finals. Portugal faced Germany, who got the first two goals in fairly quick succession, the first from Bastian Schweinsteiger on 22 minutes and the second four minutes later from Miroslav Klose. The Portuguese were in shock, but managed to pull themselves together just before half-time as Nuno Gomes knocked in the rebound from a Cristiano Ronaldo shot (Ronaldo was 23 and appearing at his second European Championship). Germany reasserted their control on the hour mark, when Michael Ballack made it 3-1, although it finished 3-2 thanks to an 87th minute Hélder Postiga goal. Portugal were a talented bunch, but hadn't really gelled, whereas Germany were finding their form at just the right time.

It was widely agreed that Croatia versus Turkey was one of the dullest matches of the tournament. Croatia had a couple of shots, but after 90 minutes it was still 0-0, so it went to extra-time. After another 28 minutes it was still 0-0 and everyone was contemplating penalties, until, after 29 minutes of extra-time, Luka Modrić set up Ivan Klasnić, who scored. That surely had to be the winner – except Turkey made one final last-ditch effort to find the back of the net and Semih Şentürk scored after two minutes of added time. On a high, the Turks won the ensuing penalty shoot-out 3-1, but the Croats were absolutely devastated.

Russia, managed by Dutchman Guus Hiddink, faced the Netherlands, managed by another Dutchman, Marco van Basten. Russia also had the mercurial Andrey Arshavin, who couldn't play in the first stage of the competition due to a red card from the qualifiers, and in truth they rather ran rings round the Dutch. They won 3-1, but only after extra-time, having made rather heavy weather of it.

Croatia's Luka Modric is challenged by René Aufhauser of Austria during the UEFA EURO 2008 Group B match at Ernst Happel Stadion on June 8, 2008

THE HISTORY OF THE EUROPEAN CHAMPIONSHIP

Spain's Andrés Iniesta challenges Yuri Zhirkov of Russia during the UEFA EURO 2008 Group D match at Stadion Tivoli Neu on June 10, 2008

Spain versus Italy threatened to make Croatia versus Turkey look entertaining. Italy's Pirlo was suspended, which didn't help matters, but the game was largely incident-free and, after 90 minutes, goal-free, so it went to extra-time and then penalties, ending 4-2 with Spain the victors.

In the semi-finals, Turkey had to play Germany. The Turkish team had been destroyed by injury – they had hardly any bodies on the bench and apparently manager Fatih Terim seriously considered using his second keeper as an outfield sub – but after 22 minutes they went ahead. It was a strange goal. German defender Philipp Lahm wasn't paying attention, Colin Kazim-Richards (born in London but eligible to play for Turkey through his mother) hit the bar and then Uğur Boral got the rebound over the line.

Turkey didn't keep the lead for long, as Schweinsteiger equalised four minutes later. It was an absorbing spectacle, but nothing quite worked for Germany after that and it stayed at 1-1 until the last ten minutes, when Klose broke the deadlock. That prompted a response from Turkey and Semih bested Per Mertesacker to slide a shot past Jens Lehmann in the German goal. The Germans couldn't leave it there, though, and on 90 minutes Lahm, arguably at fault for both Turkish goals, blasted it past Rüştü Reçber. The Turks couldn't come back from that – apart from anything else they had run out of time – and it ended 3-2 to Germany.

Unfortunately, the second semi-final didn't deliver quite such an edge-of-the-seat experience. The first half was frankly dull, with Russia, particularly Arshavin, unrecognisable from their previous tournament outings and Spain failing to play with verve or vigour. After the break, the Spanish took the bull by the horns, though. Xavi and Andrés Iniesta combined to engineer a goal for Xavi; Dani Güiza scored from a neat little Cesc Fàbregas pass; and Iniesta and Fàbregas worked a goal for David Silva. Spain won 3-0.

2008 FINAL — Spain 1-0 Germany

It wasn't necessarily a great final. Like the 2008 tournament itself, it had its moments, but also its mistakes. One came in the first minute when Spain's Sergio Ramos didn't look where he was passing to and gave the ball to Germany's Klose, who, fortunately for the Spanish, was hustled into running it off the pitch by Carles Puyol before he had a chance to do something constructive with it. There was another after half an hour or so, when Lahm failed to contain Fernando Torres and Lehmann, known for the occasional rash decision, sprinted off his line, allowing Torres to gently dink the ball over him.

Spain took the lead and control of the game, continuing to physically intimidate the Germans — Silva should have been sent off after for a head-butt on Podolski, but wasn't even booked — and gradually reducing their opponents' share of the possession. Germany's best chance came 15 minutes into the second half, when Schweinsteiger brought the ball down to set up Ballack, but although his shot was powerful, it went just wide of the goal. It stayed at 1-0 to Spain and that was the final scoreline. The Spanish had exhibited skill and strength, and were deserving winners of an extremely enjoyable competition with many memorable moments.

MAGIC MOMENTS
POETRY IN MOTION

For Germany's first quarter-final goal against Portugal, Lukas Podolski ran down the left, swapping quick passes with Miroslav Klose and Michael Ballack. Arriving at the byline, he dodged two Portuguese defenders and timed his cross perfectly for Bastian Schweinsteiger, who came charging in and stabbed it home past Ricardo. It was the goal of the tournament.

The Spanish players celebrate winning the 2008 Euros by beating Germany 1-0, June 29, 2008

THE HISTORY OF THE EUROPEAN CHAMPIONSHIP

EURO 2012

POLAND | UKRAINE

The 2012 tournament in Poland and Ukraine had a familiar look to it. Of the 16 countries that had competed in 2008, 12 had returned, along with England, Denmark, the co-hosts Ukraine and, after 24-year absence, the Republic of Ireland. Reigning champions Spain, who had gone on to a World Cup triumph in 2010, were still the team to beat. Netherlands or Germany, were considered the likeliest to do that, but even they would need to find some great form.

The group games threw up a jumble of results, which made the final matches tense and exciting. Rivals Poland and Russia met in Warsaw in a gripping, end-to-end contest. Twenty-two goal attempts resulted in a 1-1 draw, with Jakub Blaszczykowski's thunderous equaliser for the hosts igniting the tournament. Portugal were two up against Denmark before Nicklas Bendtner's second headed goal in the 80th minute evened up the scores. Silvestre Valera then won it for the Portuguese with three minutes left.

England versus Sweden featured terrible defending and high drama. England took the lead through Andy Carroll, but by the hour Sweden had established a lead. England substitute Theo Walcott changed the game. He scored his first international goal for four years before setting up Danny Welbeck's instinctive back-flick winner. In contrast, Spain's 4-0 demolition of Ireland was just a perfect display of controlled tiki-taka passing and devastating finishing – all achieved without a designated striker.

The final group games saw both host nations exit the tournament along with two pointless teams in the out-of-their-depth Republic of Ireland and a dismally underperforming Netherlands. Everyone else scrapped for a knock-out

Cristiano Ronaldo scores Portugal's first goal during the EURO 2012 quarter final match against Czech Republic, at The National Stadium on June 21, 2012

THE HISTORY OF THE EUROPEAN CHAMPIONSHIP

spot. Greece, surprisingly, ousted the dark horses Russia; Germany notched a third group victory over Denmark which also helped Italy through; a scintillating Cristiano Ronaldo double-doomed the Netherlands at the hands of Portugal; Wayne Rooney returned from suspension to score the only goal as England defeated Ukraine; and France went through at Sweden's expense, despite being losing to them as Zlatan Ibrahimović hit an amazing scissor-kick volley from the edge of the area.

The first quarter-final was the Cristiano Ronaldo show. The 27-year-old Portuguese phenomenon tormented the toothless Czechs. He hit the woodwork twice before finding the net with 12 minutes remaining, thumping a header into the ground and past keeper

Thiago Motta (C) of Italy is surrounded by Toni Kroos (L), Bastian Schweinsteiger (2nd L) and Philipp Lahm (R) of Germany during the UEFA EURO 2012 semi final match at National Stadium on June 28, 2012

Petr Čech. Germany put an end to another Greek miracle with a 4-2 victory, while Spain's seemingly unstoppable journey to the final continued as they waltzed past an ineffectual France. Finally, Italy, with Andrea Pirlo purring, took on a limited but determined England. Totally outplayed, England somehow clung on until Alessadro Diamanti sealed the penalty shoot-out.

For once the semi-finals had delivered the four best teams in the tournament. The imperious Spain had a team of stars around the mesmerising Andrés Iniesta and Xavi in midfield. Germany had fulfilled their promise with Philipp Lahm and Mats Hummels excelling in defence and an in-form Bastian Schweinsteiger, with Marco Reus and Mesut Özil in midfield. Italy's coach Cesare Prandelli had utilised the masterful Pirlo and a brooding Balotelli, while Portugal had been propelled by the genius of Ronaldo, with João Moutinho in best supporting role.

When Spain faced their Iberian rivals Portugal in their semi-final, their smooth-running machine faltered. Harried at every step by their opponents, for the first time in the competition they failed to click. The game was reduced to moments of individual brilliance. Xavi caused problems with his dribbling, while Ronaldo ran at the Spanish defence and flashed free-kicks just wide. Spain finished extra-time on top, but could not break the deadlock. In the shoot-out both Moutinho and Bruno Alves missed for Portugal, leaving Fàbregas to drill home the winner. Ronaldo, an unused fifth penalty-taker, looked on as Spain celebrated.

In the other semi-final Germany initially looked like ending their international hoodoo against the Italians. Pirlo cleared off his own line, Andrea Barzagli went perilously close to scoring an own goal and Buffon saved well from Toni Kroos. Then, after 20 minutes, came a long pass from Pirlo, a cross from Antonio Cassano and Balotelli rose to head in for Italy. Germany brought the best out of Buffon, but before half-time Balotelli struck again. He chased a long ball and, reaching the edge of the area, smashed a shot into the top corner. Germany threw everything at Italy in the second half, but their only reward was a fortunate penalty converted by Özil in added time.

Mario Balotelli (C) of Italy celebrates with team-mates Claudio Marchisio (L) and Daniele De Rossi after scoring his team's second goal during the UEFA EURO 2012 semi final match against Germany at the National Stadium on June 28, 2012

THE HISTORY OF THE EUROPEAN CHAMPIONSHIP

2012 FINAL — Spain 4-0 Italy

Spain, in all their tiki-taka glory, were at the peak of their powers in 2012. During the tournament, their possession-greedy style had been slated by many as boring, even claiming it was used as a defensive strategy. In the final at the Olympiyskiy Stadium in Kyiv, they gave the most emphatic retort possible with an irresistible display of passing, moving and deadly creativity.

Italy were the surprise team of the tournament. Cesare Prandelli won plaudits for getting the best from a limited Italian squad. Gianluigi Buffon proved he was still among the world's top keepers; Georgio Chiellini and Leonardo Bonucci were solid in defence; Daniele De Rossi shone as a libero; the playmaker Pirlo was at his masterful best; and even the volatile Balotelli kept the headlines to his goals.

Spain set up without any strikers – just four defenders and six midfielders, of whom only defensive cover Sergio Busquets held his position. Xabi Alonso, David Silva, Xavi, Iniesta and Fàbregas were constantly interchanging positions. Prandelli had seen how the Germans had blunted them, but Spanish coach Vicente del Bosque's switch from attacking through the centre to utilise the wings left Italy grasping air.

MAGIC MOMENTS

PEERLESS PIRLO

At 33 years old, Andrea Pirlo was the best thing about Euro 2012 that wasn't Spanish. His spot-kick against England was pure class. At 3-2 down in the shoot-out and with England keeper Joe Hart laughing and jumping around, Pirlo stepped up and executed the coolest 'Panenka' ever – even more deft and cheeky than the original.

Spain began the match at a searing pace unseen in any of their previous games in the finals. Less than a quarter of an hour had been played, when David Silva's header from a Fàbregas cross started the rout. They had doubled the lead four minutes before the break, when Xavi's fabulous return pass left Alba clear to shoot past Buffon. They dominated possession and their intricate passing triangles had purpose; they controlled the game and suddenly changed the pace to create openings.

Italy were not complete bystanders. Cassano twice tested Spanish keeper Iker Casillas and Di Natale squandered two chances. However, unlucky with injuries and fatigue, Italy had used up their quota of substitutes when Thiago Motta tore a hamstring – he had only been on the pitch for four minutes. They were forced to play the last 30 minutes with ten men. They held out until the 84th minute when another delicious Xavi pass allowed substitute Fernando Torrres to make it 3-0. Four minutes later Torres set up another substitute, Juan Mata, who bettered West Germany's 1972 record-winning margin.

On his 100th appearance for Spain, Casillas lifted the trophy. After their Euro 2008 triumph, he became the first captain to lead a team to two Euro successes. There was no doubt they were deserved champions. Ten of their players – Buffon, Pique, Ramos, Alba, Busquets, Alonso, Silva, Xavi, Iniesta and Fàbregas – featured in the UEFA squad of the tournament with the immaculate Iniesta being named as the player of the tournament. Spain were acknowledged as being one of the finest teams of all time. They played with such flair and panache, averaging nearly 700 passes per game throughout the finals. Their tiki-taka style was criticised for being sterile and dull, and some games had supported that argument, but their masterful possession game would change the face of football for the next decade.

Spain's goalkeeper Iker Casillas lifts the trophy after the Euro 2012 final against Italy in Kiev, Ukraine, Sunday, July 1, 2012

EURO 2016

For two decades there were 16 places at the finals of the European Championship, but in 2016 UEFA enlarged it to 24. There would be six sets of four in the group stage, followed by a three-round knockout stage and final. The expansion meant that several teams who hadn't played in the tournament's finals before – Albania, Iceland, Northern Ireland and Wales – were among those who congregated in France.

In addition to the top two teams in each group, four teams who came third also went forward to the round of 16, which all meant that after 36 games had been played, just eight teams were dropped. Russia, Sweden and Turkey were among those sent straight home, while Wales, Northern Ireland and Iceland (in descending order of population size) were among those who got to stay on, at least for now.

In the first game of the next round, Poland faced Switzerland. Poland were the more energetic, but at the end of 90 minutes both teams had a goal apiece. It went to extra-time and then penalties. The Poles looked tired and likely to falter, but they pulled through, winning the shoot-out 5-4, Switzerland's Granit Xhaka sending his shot wide for the only miss.

On paper Wales versus Northern Ireland wasn't a glamour fixture and it wasn't a scintillating game in reality either, but Wales got the slightly undeserved win thanks to an own goal from the under-pressure Northern Irishman Gareth McAuley.

Portugal's talisman Cristiano Ronaldo wasn't really fit, but then Croatia's talisman Luka Modrić wasn't really fit either. Consequently, there were virtually no shots on goal until the last five minutes of extra-time when, suddenly anxious to avoid penalties, Marko Pjaca crossed to Ivan Perišić, whose header hit the post. Renato Sanches then passed to Nani, who passed to Ronaldo. His shot was blocked by Danijel Subašić, but Ricardo Quaresma caught the rebound and nodded it in. It was 1-0 to Portugal and Croatia were out.

France, drawn against Republic of Ireland, gave away a penalty after just two minutes and Robbie Brady converted it. The French seemed slightly rattled, but manager Didier Deschamps calmed them down at half-time and, just short of the hour mark, Bacary Sagna crossed to Antoine Griezmann, who scored with a header. He got another one three minutes later and that was that. There was an early goal in the Germans' game against Slovakia, too, although Jérôme Boateng waited until eight minutes had passed before netting for Germany. Mesut Özil missed a penalty, but Mario Gómez, just before half-time, and Julian Draxler, 20 minutes after it, made it 3-0.

That was a clear-cut scoreline. Belgium's 4-0 against Hungary was even more decisive. The Hungarians challenged briefly, but with goals from Toby Alderweireld, Michy Batshuayi, Eden Hazard and Yannick Carrasco, the Belgians' class was never in doubt.

Spain were not quite the side they had been and looked vulnerable at the back. Italy were ready to exploit that weakness and kept David De Gea in the Spanish goal under fairly continuous pressure. The goals came from Giorgio Chiellini and Graziano Pellè. Italy won 2-0 and Spain crashed out.

In the final match of the round, mighty England met minnows Iceland. Again, there was an early penalty. It was

Wales' forward Gareth Bale (L) runs for the ball during the Euro 2016 group B football match against England at the Bollaert-Delelis stadium in Lens on June 16, 2016

THE HISTORY OF THE EUROPEAN CHAMPIONSHIP

Switzerland's Xherdan Shaqiri's over-head goal, during the EURO 2016 round of 16 match against Poland at Stade Geoffroy-Guichard, Saint-Etienne, France on June 25, 2016

given away by goalkeeper Hannes Þór Halldórsson and Wayne Rooney slotted home, but two minutes later England were caught napping and Ragnar Sigurðsson equalised for Iceland. Then another 12 minutes after that Joe Hart in the England goal failed to save Kolbeinn Sigþórsson's soft shot. Harry Kane had a couple of misplaced attempts, but the scoreline stayed at 2-1. Iceland had got the better of England.

So 16 had been reduced to eight and as well as the names you might expect, like France and Germany, there were some unexpected sides in the mix, like Wales and Iceland. The first quarter-final saw Poland pitted against Portugal. Polish superstar Robert Lewandowski got straight to the point, scoring after two minutes, but around 30 minutes into the game, Sanches exchanged passes with Nani and equalised. The second half was eventless and it dragged on into extra-time and then penalties. Poland's Jakub Błaszczykowski was the first to miss and it ended 5-3 to Portugal.

Wales succumbed to a majestic strike from Belgium's Radja Nainggolan in the first 15 minutes of their quarter-final. However, injuries meant the Belgians were fielding two inexperienced defenders and 15 minutes later they allowed Ashley Williams to equalise. The Welsh had a real superstar in Gareth Bale, but their second goal came from Hal Robson-Kanu. Then four minutes from full-time they got their third with a bullet header from Sam Vokes. It was an upset. Belgium had botched it; Wales had battled through to the semi-finals.

Germany and Italy could have been a great quarter-final, but they more or less cancelled each other out. It was 1-1 at full-time and still 1-1 after extra-time, with Germany eventually winning 6-5 on penalties. In the last match of the round France knew they simply couldn't let Iceland win and they signalled their intent from the off, eventually scoring five, although Iceland got two back and left with their heads held high.

Come the first semi-final there was a sense that Chris Coleman's Welsh side had made it as far as they could. They seemed out of energy and ideas, and although Bale managed a couple of first-half shots they were off-target. Portugal weren't much brighter, but picked it up after the break with goals from Ronaldo and Nani – the former a strong header, the latter an opportunistic toe-poke – on 50 minutes and 53 minutes respectively.

2016 FINAL — Portugal 1-0 France (a.e.t.)

There was an incident early on in the final between hosts France and Portugal that looked as though it would change the whole course of the game. Ronaldo, receiving a pass from team-mate Cédric, was knocked to the ground by Dimitri Payet. It should certainly have been a yellow card for Payet, perhaps even a red, but the referee didn't give so much as a free-kick. Ronaldo limped off, came back on with his knee strapped up, but 20 minutes later had to be substituted for Quaresma. France were hardly shining, but surely the Portuguese couldn't succeed without their superstar?

As the second half kicked off, the French finally started to play. An out-of-form Paul Pogba volleyed over the bar, Moussa Sissoko had a shot and André-Pierre Gignac, who had replaced Olivier Giroud, hit the post, as did Griezmann in the dying seconds of added time, but, goalless, it went to extra-time. Having hung on this far without Ronaldo, Portugal now began to look more confident. Éder, who had come on for Sanches, headed in a corner from Quaresma, but Hugo Lloris in the French goal pushed it away. Éder wasn't about to give up, though, and, shrugging off Laurent Koscielny, his long-range strike powered into the corner of the net. It was 1-0 to the Portuguese.

That was the only goal of the game and, at the end of the 51-match tournament, Portugal's valiant performance had made them champions. Some complained that Euro 2016 as a whole was dull. It was true that nearly half the games were goalless at half-time and the average number of goals per game was only 2.12 – the lowest figure for a European Championship since 1980. However, all the late goals made for exciting endings to matches, some great football had still been played and, although it may not have been a classic competition, for some of the smaller teams in particular, it had been a tournament to remember.

MAGIC MOMENTS
THUNDER CLAP

They might have been first-time qualifiers, but in 2016 Iceland (population just 335,000) certainly put their mark on the tournament. Not only did the team beat England and reach the quarter-finals, but the fans really made their presence felt with their co-ordinated chanting and stadium-shaking Viking clap.

Eder of Portugal runs to celebrate his goal in extra time during the UEFA European Championship 2016 final match at the Stade de France, Paris, July 10th, 2016

THE HISTORY OF THE EUROPEAN CHAMPIONSHIP

EURO 2020

PAN-EUROPEAN/UEFA

To mark the 60th anniversary of the first European Championship, UEFA organised a special edition of the competition with the finals taking part in 11 different countries around Europe and the semis and final being held at Wembley. The tournament was delayed a year by the Covid-19 pandemic with the matches actually taking place in 2021.

The 24 qualified teams included first-timers Finland and North Macedonia with Scotland appearing in their first Euros since 1996. The groups brought plenty of entertaining matches. Denzel Dumfries headed a dramatic late winner to earn the Netherlands victory after Ukraine had come back from 2-0 down and an exciting game saw Germany storm back, aided by two own goals, to beat Portugal 4-2. This stage also featured some great goals, such as Patrik Schick's chip from the halfway line for Czech Republic against Scotland and İrfan Can Kahveci's peach of a shot for Turkey against Switzerland. It was, however, overshadowed by Denmark's Christian Eriksen suffering a cardiac arrest in their opening match.

Characterised by high-quality football, the round of 16 games were thrilling. VAR — now used for the first time in the Euros — disallowed Marko Arnautović's header, which might have seen Austria beat Italy, only for substitutes Federico Chiesa and Matteo Pessina to strike in extra-time to send the Azzurri through. Belgium put out champions Portugal; Denmark, still in shock, destroyed Wales in a 4-0 victory; the Czech Republic defeated ten-man Netherlands in the biggest surprise yet; and Raheem Sterling and

Christian Eriksen of Denmark is stretchered off of the field by team mates and medics after receiving medical treatment during the UEFA Euro 2020 Group B match between against Finland on June 12, 2021

THE HISTORY OF THE EUROPEAN CHAMPIONSHIP

Harry Kane struck late for England as they ended a 55-year wait for a knockout tie victory over Germany. Two incredible matches happened on one day. A Luka Modrić-inspired Croatia scored two goals in the dying minutes to take Spain to extra-time, but lost 5-3; then the Swiss, having been seconds away from elimination, shared six goals with France, before beating the favourites on penalties.

In the quarter-finals, Spain faltered against Switzerland. Despite the Swiss having a man sent off on 75 minutes, the game ended 1-1 and Spain needed penalties to progress. A weaving run and an emphatic curling strike from Lorenzo Insigne sealed Italy's 2-1 victory over an ageing and injury-depleted Belgium. The tournament's dark horses, Denmark, overcame the Czech Republic by a similar score courtesy of a super Kasper Dolberg volley after a cross from the outside of Joakim Mæhle's boot. Meanwhile, in Rome, England showed quality and composure in a 4-0 thrashing of Ukraine, with Kane hitting a brace, a Harry Maguire header and Jordan Henderson scoring his first international goal in his 62nd appearance.

The Euro 2020 circus now descended on Wembley for the last three matches of what had been a thrilling tournament. Luis Enrique's Spain side had overcome a difficult start, but French-born defender Aymeric Laporte had led the defence and 19-year-old Pedri had been a revelation. They faced Italy, who had not tasted defeat since September 2018. With strong centre-backs Leonardo Bonucci and Giorgio Chiellini, and midfield energy in Insigne, Chiesa and Nicolo Barella, coach Mancini blended style and steel. It was a gripping tie with the two most technically gifted sides at the tournament taking turns to dominate a chess-like game. On the hour, Chiesa

Denmark's Joakim Maehle goes down after a challenge from Gareth Bale of Wales during the UEFA Euro 2020 Round of 16 match, at Johan Cruijff Arena on June 26, 2021

shimmied to beat two defenders and flighted a shot into the corner. Italy's lead lasted 20 minutes, as substitute Álvaro Morata played a one-two with Dani Olmo and slid the ball past keeper Donnarumma. Morata was a hero for less than an hour. After extra-time failed to break the deadlock, he missed Spain's vital penalty leaving Jorghino to send Italy to the final.

England had home advantage and momentum. They were still to concede a goal, winger Raheem Sterling had presented a constant danger and in Kane they had a deadly striker. However, their semi-final opponents, Denmark, had shown heart and discipline to win three consecutive matches. Left-winger Maehle had put in brilliant displays with Dolberg and Mikkel Damsgaard excellent in midfield.

It was the underdogs who struck first. Damsgaard fizzing a dipping free-kick over the wall and under Jordan Pickford's crossbar. Nine minutes later, England drew level when Simon Kjaer's desperate lunge turned Bukayo Saka's cross into his own net. Until just before half-time in extra-time a dominant home team were denied by the excellent goalkeeping of Kasper Schmeichel. Then Sterling hit the ground by the byline and won a penalty. Schmeichel even kept out Kane's spot kick, but the rebound fell kindly for the striker to send England to their first international final in over half a century.

England's Harry Kane and Phil Foden celebrate Kane's goal during the UEFA Euro 2020 Semi-final match against Denmark at Wembley Stadium on July 07, 2021

THE HISTORY OF THE EUROPEAN CHAMPIONSHIP

2020 FINAL
Italy 1-1 England (a.e.t.)
(Italy won 3-2 on penalties)

Surely it was meant to be – England in a final at Wembley – and although Covid restrictions meant it wasn't a capacity crowd, there were 67,000 people inside the stadium and an estimated 328 million watching on TV. As kick-off approached the atmosphere was tense and it was tense outside, too, as thousands of ticketless fans took advantage of inadequate security and attempted to break into the ground. It was public disorder on an unprecedented scale, but fortunately neither that nor the drizzle affected the on-field focus.

England were in all-white, Italy in all-dark blue, and the game got off to a great start for the home side when Harry Kane passed to Kieran Trippier, who ran down the right and crossed to Luke Shaw, who shot low, past keeper Donnarumma, and scored his first England goal. At 1 minute and 56 seconds it was also the fastest goal ever in a Euros final. The Three Lions kept launching attacks, but after 15 minutes the Italians asserted themselves. They had most of the possession and both teams had chances, but at half-time it was still 1-0 to England.

MAGIC MOMENTS
TEARFUL ENDING

One of the enduring images from the 2020 final is manager Gareth Southgate consoling Bukayo Saka, who was in tears, having missed the final penalty of the shoot-out. At Euro 96 Southgate also missed a penalty that put England out of the tournament, so he had been in exactly the same position and knew exactly how Saka was feeling.

After the break England continued to chase that decisive second goal, while the Italians settled into a productive rhythm, their shots either going wide or being claimed by England goalie Jordan Pickford. However, in the 67th minute Italy won a corner. Pickford turned the ball away, but it hit the post and the rebound was knocked in by Leonardo Bonucci, who, at 34 years and 71 days old, became the oldest scorer in a Euros final.

Just before full-time the match was stopped briefly so a pitch invader could be removed, but after 90 minutes it was still 1-1 and it went to extra-time. Attacks from both sides continued, but neither team could quite finish it off. This certainly wasn't where England manager Gareth Southgate wanted to be, but a penalty shoot-out was now unavoidable.

Domenico Berardi scored for Italy, as did Kane for England, so it was 1-1. Andrea Belotti was next, but Pickford saved his shot and then Harry Maguire netted firmly, so England had the advantage at 2-1. Bonucci took Italy's third to level it at 2-2, but extra-time sub Marcus Rashford hit the post, so it was still 2-2. Federico Bernardeschi made it 3-2, but Donnarumma saved the shot from Jadon Sancho, another late sub. If Jorginho scored Italy were home and dry, but Pickford got his hands to it. The pressure was now on 19-year-old Bukayo Saka to equalise and trigger the sudden death shoot-out, but Donnarumma went the right way and saved it. Italy were European champions.

Afterwards Italian manager Roberto Mancini said he felt his team deserved to win, while England's Southgate pointed out his team were at least consistent, having reached a World Cup semi-final in 2018 and now a Euros final. Southgate emphasised his men could be immensely proud of what they had achieved, but acknowledged they were all bitterly disappointed.

Italy's players react during the penalty shootout in the Euro 2020 final at Wembley in July 2021.